Understanding and Applying Critical Policy Study

Reading Educators Advocating for Change

Jacqueline Edmondson
Pennsylvania State University
University Park, Pennsylvania, USA

INTERNATIONAL
Reading Association
800 BARKSDALE ROAD, PO BOX 8139
NEWARK, DE 19714-8139, USA
www.reading.org

The International Reading Association attempts, through its publications, to provide a forum for a wide spectrum of opinions on reading. This policy permits divergent viewpoints without implying the endorsement of the Association.

Director of Publications   Joan M. Irwin
Editorial Director, Books and Special Projects   Matthew W. Baker
Managing Editor   Shannon Benner
Permissions Editor   Janet S. Parrack
Acquisitions and Communications Coordinator   Corinne M. Mooney
Associate Editor, Books and Special Projects   Sara J. Murphy
Assistant Editor   Charlene M. Nichols
Administrative Assistant   Michele Jester
Senior Editorial Assistant   Tyanna L. Collins
Production Department Manager   Iona Muscella
Supervisor, Electronic Publishing   Anette Schütz
Senior Electronic Publishing Specialist   Cheryl J. Strum
Electronic Publishing Specialist   R. Lynn Harrison
Proofreader   Elizabeth C. Hunt

Project Editor   Sara J. Murphy

Cover Design   Linda Steere

Copyright 2004 by the International Reading Association, Inc.
All rights reserved. No part of this publication may be reproduced or transmitted in any form or by any means, electronic or mechanical, including photocopy, or any information storage and retrieval system, without permission from the publisher.

Web addresses in this book were correct as of the publication date but may have become inactive or otherwise modified since that time. If you notice a deactivated or changed Web address, please e-mail books@reading.org with the words "Website Update" in the subject line. In your message, specify the Web link, the book title, and the page number on which the link appears.

Library of Congress Cataloging-in-Publication Data
Edmondson, Jacqueline, 1967-
   Understanding and applying critical policy study : reading educators advocating for change / Jacqueline Edmondson.
      p. cm.
   Includes bibliographical references and index.
   ISBN 0-87207-544-3 (pbk.)
   1. Education--Political aspects--United States. 2. Education--Social aspects--United States. 3. Education and state--United States. I. Title.
   LC89.E24 2004
   379.73--dc22
                                                                        2004001113

For my dad,
James Russell Zehring

CONTENTS

ACKNOWLEDGMENTS

Thank you to the many teachers who helped me to think about this book in different ways, among them Ellen Campbell, Robin Fillman, Kelly Hastings, Cynthia Lee, Doug Morris, Chris Robbins, David Rockower, Anne Slonaker, Pam Solvie, Rich Wykoff, and especially Patrick Shannon.

Thank you to Matt Baker at the International Reading Association for his patience and insightful guidance with this project. Thank you as well to Sara Murphy for her thoughtful and careful editing work and attention to the details of this manuscript.

Finally, as always, my love and deep appreciation to Michael, Jacob, and Luke.

Even in the darkest times we have the right to expect some illumination, and that such illumination may well come less from theories and concepts than from the uncertain, flickering, and often weak light that some men and women, in their lives and their works, will kindle under almost all circumstances and shed over the time span that was given them on earth. (Arendt, 1968, p. ix)

Some educators may characterize the current contexts for language and literacy education in U.S. public schools to be "dark times." The increased attention to standards and high-stakes testing, the growing scrutiny of teachers and teacher education through teacher testing policies, the linking of education funding and military recruitment, the decreased money for infrastructure and programmatic needs while student populations are increasing in number and diversity, and other such trends may seem for some educators to be insurmountable problems. Yet, there are teachers who have worked to variously deflect, co-opt, and change policies in ways that make spaces for the kind of education they know to be best for their students. However, their stories are not often told publicly. Most policy studies are conducted by an outside observer who decides on the "goodness of fit" a policy has for a particular situation, and rarely do these studies include teacher voices in their account. This is not the case with the policy study in this book. Instead, this book considers teachers who are engaged with policy—first within the context of research conducted by Shirley Brice Heath and teachers in her community in the 1970s, and second in the stories three educators offer about their teaching in recent years. These stories are of and by teachers working in "dark times," and the stories offer insight and hope that teachers' circumstances can and will be different.

Contexts of This Book

Current federal policies in education in the United States have their roots in the remnants of the Cold War and Civil Rights movement of the 1960s, as well as the capitalistic and business influences that drove President George H.W. Bush's America 2000 plan and the Clinton administration's education-related legislation through the late 1980s and early 1990s. My own first vivid recollection of federal education policy comes from this time when the popular press and media directed attention toward the concern that the United States was at risk because of the quality (or lack thereof) of public education (see National Commission on Excellence in Education, 1983, for an example of such a publication). Then in 1989, as a brand new teacher, I received a small red, white, and blue pamphlet in my school mailbox. The pamphlet, tucked in with the announcement for Back to School Night and the fire alarm testing schedules, included a list of then-President George H.W. Bush's new education initiative, America 2000. I remember reading the list of goals, which included statements about academic standards, graduation rates, achievement tests, and teacher education, then tossing the pamphlet in the nearest trashcan. Nice ideas, I thought, but what does Bush know about teaching? And what do his policies have to do with me? I gathered my mail, grabbed a cup of coffee, and went down the hall to meet my kindergarten students, children who would be graduating from high school by the time America 2000 was to be realized.

As a young teacher, I was not sure that policy, particularly federal policy, had much to do with my work. Politics seemed to be for the rich and famous, and I was neither. I figured I would go to my classroom each day, close my door, and teach my students in the ways I knew they needed, a stance shared by many of my fellow teachers. Of course, in my naiveté, I did not realize that closing my door was, in fact, a political act. It was not until years later, when I was in graduate school, that I learned from education professor Patrick Shannon that my teaching always involved my own or someone else's vision for how we should live together, and whether I acknowledged it or not, someone's policies, someone's values were always operating in and around the classrooms where I taught. Whether the policies were about who parked in which space in the parking lot, whether school would be cancelled because of falling snow, or how much I would pay to the local public library in fines when I returned late my kindergarten students' favorite book, someone's ideas about how we would carry on in this place called *school* prevailed.

As my ideas about policy have changed, I've considered how the ideas we as educators have about policies and schools are influenced by the circumstances and contexts in which we teach. Often, the teachers who enter my graduate school classes begin to talk about the No Child

Left Behind Act of 2001, testing policies, and standards, and they frequently ask, How did it come to this? As we work together to lay out a progression of policies and political influences, they discuss their own understandings of policies and inevitably turn to questions such as, What can we do? As they share their insights, concerns, and hopes, I am reminded of the words of Karl Marx (1852/1963): "[People] make their own history, but they do not make it just as they please; they do not make it under circumstances chosen by themselves, but under circumstances directly found, given, and transmitted from the past" (p. 15).

Many ideas about literacy and literacy education that we have as teachers reflect the aims and ideologies of the times in which we live, which in turn have been given to us from the past. We study and teach literacy in relation to contemporary schools, situations, and needs, and we experience literacy as part of a society that demands it be used and taught in particular ways and for specified purposes. For example, in the United States, the proposed need to remain dominant in a global economy has been an explicit influence in calls for improvements in literacy education, resulting in corresponding programs, policies, and teaching methods. When running for his first term as president, Bill Clinton (Clinton & Gore, 1992) claimed, "We know two things about education in our country today. It's more important to our economic well-being than ever before, and we still don't have the educational quality or opportunities that our people need" (p. 131).

Clinton believed that the key to success in school began with literacy, and he proposed the America Reads Challenge to have all children read well and independently by the third grade. His proposal brought about policy changes—most notably the Reading Excellence Act of 1998 and its emphasis on reliable and replicable research, along with a search for research-based pedagogy—which were put in place to ensure that all children in the United States learned to read (see National Institute of Child Health and Human Development [NICHD], 2000). Other groups extended this principle, perhaps most notably the Center for the Improvement of Early Reading Achievement (CIERA). The Center's website states, "All students will read independently and well by the end of 3rd grade," attributing this quote to the U.S. President and Secretary's Priorities, U.S. Department of Education, 1997 (see www.ciera.org/about/index.html). The Center, a prestigious organization, has generated much research for teachers of young children that began with this basic assumption. For some teachers, this assumption may be unproblematic; however, such assumptions need to be carefully considered in public dialogues about schooling and literacy, and they need to be questioned if we are to try to understand why we teach the way we do, which viewpoints we are supporting (or not), and what the consequences of particular viewpoints will be. In the end, being able to critically consider policy and its assumptions will help us all to become better teachers because these understandings will raise our awareness of the work we are doing in school, allowing us to be savvier about the conditions and purposes of education in U.S. public schools.

Purpose of This Book

It is the purpose of this book to critically consider the influences and contexts of literacy education and policy, to discuss where policies have originated and why, and to consider how policies can be either preserved or changed. To do so, we will engage in critical policy study, which emphasizes the points in Marx's previously cited quote by asking what the histories and circumstances are that influence how and why we teach literacy in particular ways. These understandings are then used to imagine how we can teach differently in the future. This undertaking is complex, to say the least, and this book is offered not as a comprehensive analysis of all policies, but instead as an introduction to policy study for teachers and others interested in education policy and as one of the many possible explanations to help address questions concerning what is going on in our schools and why. It is my hope that teachers who read this book will begin to make sense of the policies that influence their work and, in turn, gain confidence that they can enter the policy arena with an understanding of where policies have originated, what policies mean, and what the possible consequences of policies will be. This book should be used as a tool and reference to begin to critically question and think about policy and policy study, and recommendations for further readings are offered in the appendix (pages 98–102) for those who wish to pursue more in-depth study of policy and policy analysis.

Of course, my interpretation of policy is but one perspective, influenced like any perspective by the times in which I live, the studies that I have done, and my own efforts to influence policy and policymaking. I welcome readers to carefully consider the arguments and analysis, and to engage in discussion around the questions asked by teachers in my graduate classes, namely, Why are things the way they are? What can we do?

To approach these questions, we must look back to early influences on policy and examine policies in relation to key critical policy study questions such as the following (Edmondson, 2000):

- Where has the policy come from? What are the social, political, and historical aspects of the policy? How are key aspects defined?
- Who are the policymakers? What are the values of the policy-makers? Why was the policy initiated?
- What are the consequences of the policy?
- Who benefits from the policy? Who is left out?

Each question is addressed within the chapters of this book as it relates to particular teachers' work in and around policy. In addition to these questions, the chapters offer explanations of trends and issues related to contemporary literacy policies, including discussions of scientifically based research and business's influence on schools.

Overview of This Book

This book is organized around teachers' concerns about policy's impact on literacy education. After chapter 1, which provides some initial definitions and an overview of policymaking and policy study, the chapters are organized first around the concerns of teachers in Heath's (1983) research, and then around stories from elementary school teachers in suburban, urban, and rural communities. Some teachers from Heath's examples and others from my own experiences actively worked to change policy by attending school board and town meetings, talking to parents and other teachers, negotiating school and community space, and so on. Others quietly subverted federal and state policies that made no sense in their classrooms, with their students. These stories teach us much about the historical, sociological, and anthropological origins and influences on policy. Each chapter, beginning with chapter 2, ends with a section titled "Policy Lessons: Implications for Teachers." These lessons are important because they make explicit some of the key points we might learn from these stories, and these implications help us to understand the possibilities for us to initiate policy changes in the future.

I have chosen to situate the historical discussion in chapter 2 within the context of Heath's work in *Ways With Words: Language, Life, and Work in Communities and Classrooms* (1983). Heath's research, conducted in rural and urban communities in the Piedmont region of North Carolina, USA, illuminates important aspects of policy that offer lessons to us today. From a historical perspective, this study provides us with a look at initial responses by educators to Civil Rights legislation and the Elementary and Secondary Education Act (ESEA) of 1965. In addition, considering Heath's work also provides policy lessons to today's educators about the importance of careful study and local responses to policy.

In chapter 3, Dan Roberts, a teacher in a suburban Pennsylvania school, explains his efforts to control the language arts components of his class. During the year that he describes, administrators, under increasing pressure to demonstrate student success in reading through improved standardized test scores, encouraged teachers to discontinue silent reading time and to instead focus efforts on preparing students for state tests. The chapter describes how Mr. Roberts worked against such policies and recommendations.

Chapter 4 is based on the story of a Detroit public charter school teacher, Rob Charleson. Mr. Charleson was expected to align his teaching philosophy with business practices and to engage his students in a Job Corps program in his school. Infiltrated with neoliberal rhetoric that casts children as "human capital" and schools as training grounds for employment, the Job Corps program required students in his elementary school to hold positions in the cafeteria, school store, and office, or to work as janitors. The chapter explains the values embedded in such policy and Mr. Charleson's resistance to the policy.

Chapter 5 questions the consequences of current education policies. Carmen Reed, a Title I teacher from a rural Pennsylvania school, explains how her day is structured and by whom, which raises important questions about who is served by particular policies. The rigid requirements expected by Ms. Reed's school administrators caused her to attempt to change school policy because of her dissatisfaction with the effects the policy implementation had on the students in her school. The chapter describes her efforts to change policy, along with her suggestions for other teachers who may be in similar circumstances.

Chapter 6 summarizes the key themes and trends that are presented throughout the book and turns toward questions about what can be done to influence policy. Although there are no all-encompassing explanations of what can be done in every policy circumstance, we can consider lessons from the teachers whose stories appear in this book as we engage in the hopeful practice of considering what the future might be. How is it that critical policy study might lead to the kindling of lights in these "dark times"?

The appendix (pages 97–104) should serve as a resource for those who wish to pursue policy study in more detail. I provide lists of suggestions for further reading, professional organizations and education advocacy groups, and websites and online publications on policy and policymaking.

Glossary of Key Terms

To begin, it seems useful to present a glossary of key terms that are important to the policy study conducted in this book. This glossary is meant to serve as an overview for readers, to guide those who are less familiar with the language of critical policy study. The definitions are intended to introduce the terms and not to indicate a simplistic or narrow representation of the concepts that are reflected by them. Although definitions of the following terms will vary depending on the context, the explanations offered here are consistent with their use in this book:

A Nation At Risk: This report, published by the U.S. Department of Education's National Commission on Excellence in Education in 1983, often is considered to be the impetus for current education reform efforts. It warned of a "rising tide of mediocrity" (p. 1) that threatened the U.S.'s position in relation to the world. The Commission recommended more stringent graduation requirements, higher standards, and changes to the teaching profession, among other points. In 1998, a follow-up report, called *A Nation Still At Risk* (Bennett et al., 1999), was published with similar conclusions and recommendations. The full text of *A Nation At Risk* can be accessed online at www.ed.gov/pubs/NatAtRisk/risk.html. The full text of *A Nation Still At Risk* can be accessed online at www.policyreview.org/jul98/nation.html.

America 2000/Goals 2000: Originally written as America 2000 in 1990 during the George H.W. Bush administration by a governor's panel that included then-governors Bill Clinton of Arkansas and Richard Riley of South Carolina among others, the policy listed goals for all U.S. school-children to achieve by the year 2000. The legislation created incentives and support to encourage state governments and local school districts to move their students toward the U.S. government's neoliberal vision of higher standards and higher academic achievement.

America Reads Challenge: The America Reads Challenge was a federal initiative introduced by President Clinton in 1996. The primary goal of the program was to teach all children to read independently by the end of the third grade. The policy relied largely on volunteer tutors, and its original conceptualization had five key components: (1) America's Reading Corps, (2) Parents as First Teachers Challenge grants, (3) Head Start expansion, (4) expansion of federal work study programs, and (5) accountability of results. (See Edmondson, 2000, for a detailed case study of America Reads.)

***Becoming a Nation of Readers*:** In 1985, the Commission on Reading offered a report (Anderson, Hiebert, Scott, & Wilkinson, 1985) that explains reading as a constructive, fluent, strategic, motivated, and lifelong pursuit. Similarly, the report explains emergent literacy and parents' important role in the process of children learning to read. Among the Commission's recommendations is the importance of silent reading to beginning readers.

conservatism: As a political ideology, conservatism emphasizes tradition and resistance to change, tolerance of inequality, and protection of the right to accumulate property. Most typically, conservatism is a reaction to a trend, policy, or phenomenon in society. It reflects a commitment to the protection of local values and beliefs, which in literacy education includes control of textbooks and a focus on hierarchical, systematic skill instruction as a "neutral" procedure. (See Shannon, 2000, for more information.)

critical policy study: This approach to policy study involves a recognition that policy is historically and socially situated, and imbued with the values of its authors. Such analysis poses questions that examine the social, political, historical, and economic realities that define and shape policy in particular contexts. Key questions for study might include,

Where has this policy come from? Who has authored the policy? Whose values are reflected in the policy? Who benefits from the policy? Who is left out of the policy?

deskilling of teachers: Attempts to control teachers through textbooks and programs that have predetermined sets of goals, predesigned lessons, and implications for classroom management change teachers' instruction away from that which requires them to create lessons for students and toward a role that expects they will "run the textbook technology during lessons" (Shannon, 1990, p. 153). This phenomenon has been referred to as "deskilling" (Shannon, 1989, p. 78) and "reskilling" (p. 82).

Elementary and Secondary Education Act (ESEA): Originally authorized in 1965 during President Lyndon B. Johnson's war on poverty, the ESEA was intended to guarantee equal opportunity for children in U.S. public schools. The original legislation included funds for Title I programs and Head Start programs, which were intended to help poor children increase their chances of doing well in school. This legislation has been reauthorized during different presidential administrations to align it with the values of the various groups that have been in power in the United States. The most recent reauthorization is George W. Bush's No Child Left Behind Act of 2001.

Fourteenth Amendment of the U.S. Constitution: This amendment was ratified on July 9, 1868. It is responsible in part for Civil Rights legislation because of the expressed need to guarantee all U.S. citizens equal protection under the law. Section 1 of the amendment, which is most relevant to the discussion in this book, reads as follows:

> All persons born or naturalized in the United States and subject to the jurisdiction thereof, are citizens of the United States and of the State wherein they reside. No State shall make or enforce any law which shall abridge the privileges or immunities of citizens of the United States; nor shall any State deprive any person of life, liberty, or property, without due process of law; nor deny to any person within its jurisdiction the equal protection of the laws.

The full text of the U.S. Constitution can be found online at www.archives.gov/national_archives_experience/constitution.html.

functionalism: This is the most prevalent type of policy analysis. Functionalism focuses on "what works" or the effects of a program or policy as it fits within an already existing system. DeMarrais and LeCompte (1990) provide an especially readable explanation of functionalism in relation to school systems.

human agency: Human agency involves "the power to *do* something" (Nealon & Giroux, 2003, p. 193), which may include struggle, resistance, and transformation. It is sometimes realized in moments of self-reflection, mediation, or active participation in societal structures, or in a refusal to participate in something. Human agency is always enabled or constrained by the contexts in which we live and work (see Giroux, 2001a, and Nealon & Giroux, 2003, for more in-depth discussion of human agency).

human capital: As an agenda of the Clinton administration, human capital refers to investment in the skills of U.S. citizens, enabling workers to move from one job to the next as needed in light of the global economy. Human capital is grounded in the belief that the strength of the nation (particularly the economy) relies primarily on the strength and skills of the people. As former President Clinton and former Vice President Al Gore were campaigning for their first term in office, they published a book titled *Putting People First: How We Can All Change America* (1992) that outlined their human capital agenda. Another explanation of the term can be found in Marshall Smith's work (see Smith & Scoll, 1995).

ideology: Aronowitz (1988) has explained that ideologies (rather than ideology) are a type of discourse with special languages, rules, and values that establish parameters for people's values and beliefs. However, he argues that ideologies are not completely determinate of people's understandings and beliefs, and the effects of ideologies are never completely predictable. There are conflicts and contradictions within ideologies, and as they compete to define truth, they often match the social, political, or economic power of the groups who accept them (see also Eagleton, 1991). Allington (2002) notes that ideology, not research or any other factor, has influenced the agendas and reports that have resulted in federal literacy policies, especially in recent years.

Improving America's Schools Act: This act is the Clinton administration's 1994 reauthorization of the ESEA. Largely considered to include the most significant changes in the ESEA from its original passage in 1965 up to this particular reauthorization, the Improving America's Schools Act included an emphasis on early literacy through Title I and Even Start programs, professional development for teachers, technology, bilingual education, 21st Century Community Learning Centers, and more. Title X, Part C, included provisions for charter schools (see chapter 4 for more details).

liberalism: This political ideology values enlightenment ideals that knowledge will bring freedom. To liberals, science is the best knowledge maker. Also, liberals believe that literacy is a basic human right and people must search for the right method of teaching literacy skills. (See Shannon, 2000, for more information.)

mobilization of bias: Any policy draws attention to some issues while detracting from others. Saunders (as cited in Clegg, 1989) says that a

> mobilization of bias...[occurs in] those situations where dominant interests may exert such a degree of control over the way in which a political system operates, and over the values, beliefs and opinions of less powerful groups within it, that they can effectively determine not only whether certain demands come to be expressed and needed, but also whether such demands will even cross people's minds. (p. 77)

neoconservatism: This political ideology shares the liberal values that no one should be restrained because of race, class, or position. It also shares the conservative belief in order, continuity, and community. Neoconservatism puts an emphasis on character and moral education that is aligned with Eurocentric values and a belief that individuals are responsible for the world, so all individuals should be equal.

neoliberalism: This is a dominant political ideology that emphasizes a focus on the growth of the economy as the primary means to address social issues. This political ideology values liberal ideas (e.g., the "free market" will solve social and public concerns) combined with conservative solutions (e.g., local control). In relation to literacy, neoliberals believe in a "reading success equation" (Edmondson & Shannon, 1998) in which learning to read well will guarantee success in school and in the job market.

No Child Left Behind Act: This act is the George W. Bush administration's reauthorized version of the ESEA. Signed in 2002, the bill continues many of the trends of education policy that were evident throughout the 1990s, including standardized testing, specifics about highly qualified teachers, and more. However, the consequences of non-compliance with the legislation are more serious than they were in any previous administration, marking a new role for the federal government in relation to U.S. public schools.

policy: Policy is an authoritative allocation of values (Ball, 1990). It has the capacity to allow or constrain movement toward particular goals and particular visions for society. Policies are intended to bring change, but they are negotiated and implemented by people across different sites and under different conditions. In the end, policy implementation is always a human endeavor, involving interpretations, decisions, and human agency as power circulates among various groups and individuals.

radical democratism: This political ideology places emphasis on redistribution of resources and recognition of groups and individuals, including those who have traditionally been disenfranchised by U.S. politics and society (see Fraser, 1996). Radical democrats ask individuals to evaluate their position in the world, respect the positions of others, and establish conditions necessary for a participatory democracy (see Shannon, 2000).

Reading Excellence Act: This legislation, passed into law in 1998, included four major goals: (1) teaching every child to read in their early childhood years, not later than the third grade; (2) improving the reading skills of students and the instructional practices of teachers through the use of findings from reliable, replicable research in reading, including phonics; (3) expanding the number of high-quality family literacy programs; and (4) reducing the number of children who are inappropriately referred to special education due to reading difficulties. The legislation caused concern among many reading researchers and educators because of the narrow definitions of reading and research (see Taylor, 1998).

resistance: Resistance is a response to domination that helps individuals and groups address oppression. Giroux's (2001b) *Theory and Resistance in Education: Toward a Pedagogy for the Opposition* offers a thorough explanation of resistance in education contexts.

CHAPTER 1

Getting Started: Developing Understandings of Policy and Policy Study

Every policy study begins from a particular viewpoint and reflects certain assumptions about what should be considered and what should be omitted. Therefore, it is important to understand at the outset the definitions and assumptions that guide the approach to the policy study.

What Is Policy?

Sociologist C. Wright Mills (1956) wrote that the powers of ordinary people are often "circumscribed by the everyday worlds in which they live, yet even in these rounds of jobs, family, and neighborhood, they often seem driven by forces they can neither understand nor govern" (p. 3). This statement seems to ring particularly true where education policymaking is concerned. As educators, we all move in and around schools, but we rarely stop to question or understand why things are the way they are. Often, the answer to this question relates to policies that work to structure our lives in particular ways. Policies are the articulation of someone's hope for the way something should be, and they are revealed through various texts, practices, and discourses that define and deliver these values (Schneider & Ingram, 1997). These articulations determine the ways in which we live together, but we are not always sure how they come to be or how we can become involved in changing them.

Policies always begin with their authors' images of an ideal society, and they are intended to be procedural and regulative statements to realize that ideal. In turn, ideals are based on values that always have social contexts and histories. Therefore, any discussion of policy must necessarily include considerations of values and ideologies, historical and social contexts, and power and prestige if it is to adequately capture the intricacies of the process. There are two general assumptions about policy throughout this book: (1) Policy is socially constructed and produced at a particular time and place and is, therefore, subject to social, economic, and political influences of the times; and (2) participants in policy events are members of various discourse groups with distinct values and interests offering a wide variety of opinions.

What Is Policymaking?

Policymaking is a dynamic process that includes the "authoritative allocation of values" (Ball, 1990, p. 3). As such, it always involves factors that make it a less-than-rational process. In other words, power, values, ideals, and personal interests all play a role in articulating what policy is and for whom it is intended. For this reason, policy is always struggled over, as it should be within any democratic society. Of late, however, policymaking seems increasingly to limit those struggles and exclude those who would dissent or offer alternative views (see Shannon, Edmondson, & O'Brien, 2002). For this reason, strategic intervention by the people for whom policy is intended, those who have been silenced in the policy process (i.e., teachers), is more important than ever.

Influencing policymaking processes is, of course, a complex matter. Legislation is never the sole product of one individual or group, and it rarely, if ever, reflects a straight "party line" (America Reads would be one exception to this norm; see Edmondson, 2000). Instead, policies reflect negotiations, values, and ideologies that cross political party lines. One recent example is liberal Senator Ted Kennedy's involvement with the No Child Left Behind Act. Kennedy did not oppose the extensive high-stakes standardized testing involved with No Child Left Behind (as other liberals, such as the late Paul Wellstone, did). His lack of opposition perhaps resulted because he shared with his brother, the late Robert Kennedy, a hope that tests would allow us to know who needs to be served through federal policies. Robert Kennedy endorsed the use of tests as part of the original ESEA in 1965, largely because he thought these tests would show that poor and minority students needed the government to intervene to improve their education (see Shannon, 1998). On the surface, conservatives share this value for accountability, but for different purposes. Their aim is not necessarily to be sure that policies serve the neediest, but instead to employ a functionalist analysis to demonstrate that policies work (or not) so that funding and resources can be directed differently (see Shannon, 2000). Shared values, in this case the belief that standardized testing can provide some "knowns" about U.S. public schooling, can bring people and groups together around particulars to formulate policies based on common interests and concerns (see also Mouffe, 1995).

Various theories and explanations exist to describe how policies are made (see Table 1). Some explanations are pluralistic in nature and expect that anyone who wants to can participate in the process (see Roller & Long, 2001, for an example of this theory in relation to reading legislation). Other explanations expect that only a handful of people, those who hold power, are able to participate in policymaking, and that the voices of others are insignificant in relation to these elite forces. For example, Tyack and Cuban (1995) propose that a policy elite have determined the model for modern schooling, and they hold that the modern emphasis on science and efficiency give policymaking the appearance of rationality. Yet other policymaking explanations focus on interest groups and their influence, or on a combination of interest and government groups.

Teachers have known the complexity of policymaking for a long time, and reading teachers often have subverted and variously deflected, for better or worse, the policies that have come their way (Fraatz, 1987). Rather than reacting to or subverting policies, however, teachers can and do become knowledgeable about policies and the corresponding values the policies represent, and in turn become more involved in influencing policy content and purposes. This approach combines pluralist theories with critical theory in order to address some of the shortcomings in typical pluralistic approaches. In other words, although pluralists might attend to issues of power, they have not necessarily focused on the values inherent in policies. Pluralism often

> assumes an "invisible hand" that guides a democratic process to produce
> policy that reflects reasonable, responsible compromises among competing

	TABLE 1
	Policymaking Models

Theory	Description
Corporate	Corporate theories explain policymaking as influenced by interest groups that become part of the decision-making and implementation system. In this way, groups help to manage society for the state or government. Corporate influences on reading policy can be found in the relationship between some textbook publishers and the federal government (see Metcalf, 2002). Philippe Schmitter (see Lehmbruch & Schmitter, 1980) is most associated with these theories.
Elite	According to this theory, policies are made by relatively small groups of influential leaders who share similar beliefs. Policy is determined by the preferences of a power elite (see Mills, 1956; see also Miliband, 1969; Tyack & Cuban, 1995). Elite influences on reading policy include the effects of panels and reports on policy. For example, the National Reading Panel's report (NICHD, 2000) influenced the content and form of the Reading First Initiative.
Group	This theory of policymaking argues that policy is a struggle among groups. Various groups (social, economic, ethnic, etc.) put pressure on the government to produce policies favorable to them. The letter-writing campaigns and calls for educators to participate in policymaking that followed the passage of the House of Representatives's version of the Reading Excellence Act are examples of pluralist attempts to influence policy (see Roller & Long, 2001). This theory is associated with work by political scientists David B. Truman (1971) and Robert A. Dahl (1967).
Subgovernment	Subgovernment theories endorse a view of policymaking whereby sections of government work with interest groups. The result is that coalitions of Congress members, bureaucracy, and interest groups develop policies around specialized areas of interest. Subgovernment theories can be found in the influence of groups such as the National Institutes of Health and the NICHD on reading policies. Hugh Heclo (1978) writes about policymaking according to this theory.

Adapted from Theodoulou, S., & Cahn, M. (1995). *Public policy: The essential readings.* Englewood Cliffs, NJ: Prentice Hall.

perspectives. Designs that are ineffective or unresponsive to public concerns are expected to result in citizen mobilizing.... If policy content is flawed, people are expected to recognize the problems and take action to bring about changes. If elites control too much power and generate policies that grant them too many advantages, countervailing groups are expected to emerge and contest these advantages. (Schneider & Ingram, 1997, p. 21)

In spite of its appeal, at least to the civic sensibilities many of us were taught in high school, pluralism is considered by some policy researchers to be ineffective in influencing policy in significant ways. Lowi (1964, 1979) argues that across the course of U.S. history, pluralism has lost power as interest groups have gained control of U.S. politics, systematically excluding particular groups (see also Newton, 1969). Due to the control that interest groups wield, critics of pluralism suggest that rational policy processes are not attainable because political leaders, rather than the general public, dominate the policymaking process. Subsequently, the resources become inequitably distributed, resulting in a cumulative political inequity (Newton, 1969). This raises significant questions about the possibilities for changing public policy in ways that attend more closely to matters of social justice.

Yet if we believe that democracy should be participatory and that as citizens we should have a voice in the policymaking process, then we must begin to overcome the limitations of pluralistic approaches. To do so, as educators, we can attend to the values and visions inherent in policy, including the power relations, in order to expose contradictions, conflicts, and shortcomings. In this way, educators can strategically and collectively work toward new and better policies. There is hope in this belief that we can unite to make changes that will bring justice and equity to public education. Part of this effort will necessarily entail educating the public—including policymakers—about matters related to public education in order to form broad coalitions around shared values and aims for children attending U.S. public schools. Critical policy study helps us to begin to understand the values and contradictions of policy.

What Is Critical Policy Study?

Policy study, like policymaking, is a political process. Its purposes and approaches are different based on the power, values, and goals of the individuals involved in the study. Generally speaking, policy study can take two forms: (1) functionalist or (2) critical (see Edmondson, 2002). Functionalist policy study engages questions of "what works" within a particular situation, keeping initial definitions and assumptions in place. Some policy researchers consider this form of policy study to be inappropriate for educational contexts because the assumptions are inimical to educational problems and issues (see Prunty, 1985). In spite of this, much policy research begins and ends with functionalist questions. Instead, this form of policy study reflects a positivist view that facts are separate from human values and ideologies, thus avoiding explicit links between education and politics. Typically, this research is policy driven, an attempt by reading researchers "to find the answers to the questions current policy makers pose in order to become recognized as the primary source of valued information" (Shannon, 1991, p. 164).

Much of the policy-driven research in reading education has focused on functionalist, methodological issues (see National Institute of Child Health and Human Development [NICHD], 2000, for one recent example), contributing to our understandings of autonomous aspects of literacy (Street, 1995). The emphasis on functionalist approaches means that much of this research has been conducted at the expense of addressing matters of social inequalities and injustices (Siegel & Fernandez, 2000) in relation to literacy and literacy education; likewise, it has avoided serious considerations of culture and power issues (Gonzalez & Melis, 2000; Street, 1995). With functionalist analyses, the role of the researcher is to assess the policy within the current structures of schools and society to determine its goodness of fit. These analyses are useful when decisions about "what is right" have been made; then, it is the role of the researcher to determine if policies move in this direction. One difficulty with this approach is that much in literacy education remains undecided, and there are important questions that need to be raised concerning what literacy education is working toward. When questions about "who benefits toward what end" are raised, then critical policy study is needed. Such policy study investigates the values in policy, policymaking, and policy implementation.

Critical policy study begins with a different set of assumptions than functionalist study. First is an understanding that educational policy is historical and political and that it always involves values and power relations. As such, there is an assumption that policy negotiations are not constructed among equals because "social, economic, and political circumstances have given certain segments of society license to assert greater influence over the outcomes" (Shannon, 1991, p. 164). Due to this assumption, critical policy analysts tend to ask questions of policy that illuminate inequalities and injustices, particularly because these questions lead them to expose contradictions. In turn, exposing contradictions allows critical policy analysts to advocate strategically for change for teachers and students.

Critical policy study is the analysis of the histories and social attachments of policy ideals. As Prunty (1985) writes, "the authoritative allocation of values draws our attention to the centrality of power and control in the concept of policy" (p. 136). Critical policy studies, then, require not only an examination of a policy's effectiveness on its own terms but also an investigation of the values embedded within it; of the images used to make the policy seem necessary and compelling; and of the real, expected, and unanticipated social consequences of the policy (Marshall, 1997). In this way, overtly political work is undertaken that exposes sources of domination and oppression with the overall goal of searching for social justice and an improvement in the human condition (Marshall, 1997; Prunty, 1985).

In the critical policy study in this book, we begin with the recognition that policy is social, and as such it has links to sociological, economic, anthropological, and historical information, raising questions about who benefits from particular policies and why. Such policy study teaches us about the complexities of policy and policymaking as we simultaneously use critical theory to look dialectically at policies in order to "decide what they offer and what they deny us" (Shannon, 1991, p. 164). To look dialectically at a policy means that we consider the historical and material forces that have worked to shape a policy's initial conception and viability within a particular societal context. It is to recognize that policies are made by people in particular times and places, and in relation to particular values and visions, and to acknowledge that power circulates through participants as policy is written and implemented in particular contexts (see Foucault, 1980). In a similar way, our analyses of policy also are conducted by people and situated in particular historical and material contexts.

Finally, this work encourages sociological imagination (Mills, 1959) and agency. That is, extending our acknowledgment that policies are social and are made by people, we recognize that they can be changed. This changing necessarily involves understanding why things are the way they are, followed by strategic imagining of how things could be otherwise. In other words, our understandings of how things could be different and our work in this direction must employ an educated hope that stresses "the contextual nature of learning, emphasizing that different contexts give rise to diverse questions, problems, and possibilities" (Giroux, 2002, p. 101). To understand these possibilities for the future, we must begin to understand the past and the policies that have led to our current legislation and education programs. For this reason, the next chapter includes a look back to the original ESEA in order to present a historical perspective concerning how that legislation has influenced current policies, particularly in reading education.

CHAPTER 2

Exploring Questions of Policy Origin: Looking Back to Move Forward

---

CRITICAL POLICY STUDY QUESTIONS ADDRESSED

Where has the policy come from?

What are the social, political, and historical aspects of the policy?

How are key aspects defined?

The purpose of this chapter is to consider policy origins. To do so, we will look back to the original Elementary and Secondary Education Act (ESEA), penned during the Johnson administration's war on poverty in the 1960s. This legislation is significant and remains important to educators today because at its inception it represented a new role for the federal government in U.S. public schools, particularly in the area of reading. Through this legislation, the U.S. government made an explicit attempt to equalize children's opportunities through education, setting the stage for subsequent legislation, including the most recent iteration of the ESEA: the No Child Left Behind Act of 2001.

The 1960s and 1970s were a time of transformation and uncertainty in many sectors of U.S. society, including public education. Prior to the 1960s, the federal government played a minimal role in U.S. schools, one that was mostly related to specific issues (such as science, math, and foreign language instruction in the context of the Cold War and National Defense Education Act) or particular programs (such as Franklin Delano Roosevelt's public work campaigns that built schools). However, the federal government's role changed dramatically in the 1960s when it committed to equalizing opportunity for disadvantaged children through education. For teachers in U.S. public schools, particularly those in the segregated South, these decades brought challenges many felt unprepared to face. Teachers and students alike experienced a "massive reshuffling" (Heath, 1983, p. 1) as schools desegregated to comply with Civil Rights legislation aiming to protect Fourteenth Amendment rights. This reshuffling was not welcome by all, particularly not by those who believed education decisions should be locally determined (see Kantor, 1991).

Within this context, Heath (1983) was engaged in preparing white teachers to teach black children and working class white children in newly desegregated classrooms how to read. Her university classes in anthropology and linguistics were filled with educators and others who hoped to better understand how to communicate with the working class and poor blacks and whites living in small communities outside of town. As she listened to her students discuss their concerns, Heath undertook a decade-long study of two rural communities in the Piedmont region of North Carolina and one "town" community. From 1969 to 1978, she "lived, worked, and played with the children and their families and friends in Trackton and Roadville" (1983, p. 5). As a researcher and educator, Heath was interested in the uses of language, both oral and written, in and across these communities as changing economic and political contexts affected the lives of community members in this region. Many of these residents commuted to town to work in the mills, and their children attended public schools in town. However, there were marked differences in the language uses found in Trackton and Roadville, as compared to those of black and white townspeople. To better understand this difference, Heath helped teachers to engage in ethnographies, to participate and observe in their schools and communities to better understand these differences themselves, and to help bridge the differences between home and school language learning and use. These teachers, in turn, engaged their students in ethnographies to likewise better understand language and its uses. The results of these studies brought different understandings of language and education and different classroom practices. Teachers began to create environments that bridged home and school literacies, and they worked with communities, businesses, and families to create curricula and learning experiences relevant to local values, concerns, and needs.

The changes these teachers and other teachers throughout the United States faced in their classrooms were largely precipitated by the Civil Rights movement and the war on poverty. This policy brought dramatic changes to U.S. public education that may not have occurred otherwise (see Prendergast, 2003, for a thorough discussion of segregation and racial justice in this time period). Of course, this policy has had many iterations, and the various reauthorizations offer insight into the dominant political values and hopes of the various eras of which it was a part. To better understand this policy and its implications in contemporary times, we will consider how it was initially defined, along with the key values and assumptions that directed this legislation across time. The key values are summarized in Table 2.

The Great Society and the Elementary and Secondary Education Act

As Heath was beginning her research in North Carolina's Piedmont region, the United States was just a few years into a new role for the federal government in public education. The ESEA, enacted in 1965 during the Civil Rights era, immediately followed federal policy about race and increasing national tension about racial inequalities throughout the 1950s. When the U.S. Supreme Court ruled in 1954 through *Brown v. the Board of Education* that racial segregation of public school children was a violation of the Fourteenth Amendment, national attention turned toward inequalities in the U.S. education system. Ratified on July 9, 1868, the Fourteenth Amendment holds that no state should make or enforce laws that

> abridge the privileges or immunities of citizens of the United States; nor shall any State deprive any person of life, liberty, or property, without due process of law; nor deny to any person within its jurisdiction the equal protection of the laws. (U.S. Constitution, amend. 14, sec. 1)

Until *Brown*, the dominant U.S. practice was to restrict access to literacy and education for blacks. State laws often made it illegal for blacks

TABLE 2
Key Political Ideologies and Related Policies

Ideology	Dominant Values (based on Shannon, 2000; Edmondson & Shannon, 1998)	Policy Examples
Conservatism	This ideology is most typically a reaction to a societal trend, policy, or phenomenon. It reflects a commitment to the protection of local values and beliefs, and the right to accumulate property. In literacy education, this includes control of textbooks and a focus on hierarchical, systematic skill instruction as a "neutral" procedure.	• No Child Left Behind Act, including the Reading First initiative
Neoconservatism	This ideology espouses liberal values that no one should be restrained because of race, class, or position. Proponents hold conservative beliefs that order, continuity, and community are important. The ideology also emphasizes character and moral education aligned with Eurocentric values and a belief that individuals are responsible for the world, so all individuals should be equal.	• Reading Excellence Act
Neoliberalism	In this ideology, liberal ideas (i.e., that the "free market" will solve social and public concerns) are combined with conservative solutions (such as local control). Proponents believe in a reading success equation, where learning to read well will guarantee success in school and later in the job market.	• America Reads Challenge • School-to-Work initiative
Liberalism	This ideology emphasizes enlightenment ideals that knowledge will bring freedom. To liberals, science is the best knowledge maker and literacy is a basic human right, so educators must search for the right method to teach literacy skills.	• Title I of the Elementary and Secondary Education Act of 1965 • *Becoming a Nation of Readers* report • *Preventing Reading Difficulties* report
Radical democratism	This ideology emphasizes recognition of all social groups and the redistribution of resources (Fraser, 1996). It encourages work through coalitions and participatory efforts to bring social change and to establish conditions for participatory democracy.	• Grassroots efforts to change policy through groups such as FairTest and publications such as those from Rethinking Schools

to learn to read. Activists such as Homer Plessy and others attempted to expose and change the social inequalities drawn along racial lines. Yet it soon became evident that any "separate but equal" tenet would never be realized, particularly in the segregated schools that young black children attended. These schools certainly were separate from but clearly never equal to white schools in a variety of aspects, including but not limited to the number of days that students attended school and the quantity and quality of resources and materials available to them.

In the years immediately preceding *Brown*, various groups and individuals carefully pointed out these inequities (see Harding, Kelley, & Lewis, 2000). Black parents in Clarendon County, South Carolina, lobbied for school bus transportation for their children (white children had several buses while their own children had none). Sixteen-year-old Barbara Rose Johns joined with the National Association for the Advancement of Colored People (NAACP) to organize a strike concerning the inadequate resources at Moton High in Farmville, Virginia. Martin Luther King, Jr.; Septima Clark; educators at the Highlander Folk School in Monteagle, Tennessee; and others similarly worked for equal rights under the law for blacks. To these plaintiffs and activists, the United States provided second-class education to blacks, denying equal education to blacks that, in turn, restricted their access to higher education and subsequent social mobility.

With the passage of *Brown*, blacks were to be afforded by law the same privileges as other U.S. citizens. Although this right was legislated, it certainly seemed an insurmountable goal given public sentiment at the time. Eighty percent of white Southerners were opposed to desegregation, and after *Brown* was passed, a "Southern manifesto" was drafted that declared that the Supreme Court could not rule on racial matters (Harding, Kelley, & Lewis, 2000). This document encouraged whites to resist the *Brown* legislation. Ninety Southern members of the U.S. House of Representatives and all but three Southern U.S. Senators— Estes Kefauver, Albert Gore, Sr., and Lyndon Johnson—signed the manifesto. President Eisenhower, in office throughout the course of these events, never made a clear public statement in support or opposition of the Supreme Court's decision, missing a key opportunity to lead the nation to peaceful social change (Harding, Kelley, & Lewis, 2000). Instead, tensions and violence throughout the United States escalated, eventually involving federal troops and military action. Perhaps one of the most publicized incidents involved the National Guard and federal troops mobilizing in Little Rock, Arkansas, to control hostile mobs when 25 black students entered Central High, integrating the 2,000-student school located in an all-white working class neighborhood.

In spite of intense controversy surrounding the legislation, *Brown* helped to set the stage for public discussion about the quality of education provided to black, poor, and disadvantaged children. During this time, education and literacy began to be cast rhetorically as "rights," an observation that has since been questioned by many prominent educators, among them Cook-Gumperz (1986), Kozol (1991), and Ladson-Billings and Tate (1995), all of whom ask in different contexts whether this right has truly been honored. Even though *Brown* was a landmark decision, it offered little change in the lived conditions for blacks in the United States (Bell, 1995) and in some cases made racism more difficult to recognize (Prendergast, 2003). Instead, *Brown* and the education legislation that followed have been considered to continue the equation between "Whiteness and literacy that had occurred for centuries by reinforcing the cultural belief in literacy as White property" (Prendergast, 2002, p. 209). Some have argued that the Supreme Court was interested only in eliminating segregation that seemed harmful to the United States within the context of the Cold War's political crisis. In other words, during a time when the United States was in competition with the Soviet Union and trying to establish itself as the "leader of the free world" (which necessarily entailed concern about human rights for people everywhere), its leaders did not want the country to be portrayed internationally as supporting the repression and oppression of black citizens (see also Dudziak, 1995; Harding, Kelley, & Lewis, 2000).

While *Brown* provided momentum for the Civil Rights movement, controversy surrounded issues of segregation and desegregation, a debate that avoided serious talk about race, institutionalized racism, and ways to eradicate these issues from the U.S. psyche. After President John F. Kennedy entered office in 1961, he proposed Civil Rights legislation, including a plan for federal aid to improve the education of poor and disadvantaged children. However, Kennedy's proposal never came to fruition, even though 65% of black children—constituting 13% of the public school population at that time—lived in poverty (Jennings, 2000). In the end, at least three key obstacles to Kennedy's proposal prevented it from becoming legislation: (1) Some feared federal aid would force integration of public schools, particularly in the South; (2) conservatives in Congress resisted federal control of public schools, arguing instead for local control; and (3) Catholic and other private schools blocked legislation that did not provide aid to them as well (Jennings, 2000).

In 1964, President Lyndon B. Johnson signed the Civil Rights Act, claiming that its passage would honor Kennedy's memory. This legislation made segregation in public facilities of any kind illegal, and although it stopped short of enacting voters' rights legislation, it laid the groundwork for later affirmative action legislation. President Johnson proposed that the United States should become a Great Society, one resting on "abundance and liberty for all," one that "demands an end to poverty and racial injustice" (Johnson, 1964, n.p.). He characterized the Great Society as "a place where every child can find knowledge to enrich his mind and to enlarge his talents" (n.p.). Reflecting the dominant liberal ideology of the time, this proposal embodied a hope that, given the right circumstances, all children could learn and U.S. citizens could overcome poverty through education. This belief in the American Dream, the hope that all those who live in the United States will be able to achieve material and other success through their own efforts, relied on education as the starting place for this achievement (Hochschild, 2001).

Coupled with the focus on education was an inherent liberal belief that the social sciences could change society and social ills. Although it was not explicitly mentioned in the Great Society legislation, Johnson recognized a need to address racial inequality in the United States. When he offered a commencement speech at Howard University in 1965, Johnson

> pointed out that "despite the court orders and the laws" the majority of African Americans continued to live in "another nation" and [he] called for solutions to the problem of black poverty that coupled antidiscrimination legislation with other programs to foster economic equality. (Kantor & Lowe, 1995, p. 6)

To Johnson and other key political players after *Brown*, racial inequality would be lessened through desegregation, and education would help to level the playing field. Up to this time, education had been primarily

"White property" (Prendergast, 2002), and it was believed that increased attention to educational opportunities—access to this "property"—would bring about a more equitable society. Yet rhetoric of a "literacy crisis" slowed the progress of the Civil Rights movement as "the discussion about improving the conditions of African American lives was displaced by laments over declining literacy standards" (Prendergast, 2002, p. 4). Furthermore, contradictions in the ideology of the American Dream were evident. On the one hand, there was a shared belief that everyone has the right to pursue success but only a few deserve to win. This belief was coupled with the central paradox of the American Dream—that "one generation's finish is the next generation's start" (Hochschild, 2001, p. 37)—making it an increasingly difficult if not impossible dream for many minority and poor children to realize.

The ESEA was a cornerstone of the Great Society. The ESEA was a complex piece of legislation, containing various Titles (called Chapters during the Reagan administration) that address different aspects of public education (see Figure 1 for a list and short descriptions of the Titles). It included categorical aid to disadvantaged children through Title I programs in reading and mathematics, Head Start programs for preschool children, funds for the purchase of library books, supplemental education centers, and the development of state departments of education.

FIGURE 1
The Elementary and Secondary Education Act of 1965: List of Titles

Title I:	Improving the Academic Achievement of the Disadvantaged
Title II:	Preparing, Training, and Recruiting High-Quality Teachers and Principals
Title III:	Language Instruction for Limited English Proficient and Immigrant Students
Title IV:	21st Century Schools
Title V:	Promoting Informed Parental Choice and Innovative Programs
Title VI:	Flexibility and Accountability
Title VII:	Indian, Native Hawaiian, and Alaskan Native Education
Title VIII:	Impact Aid Program
Title IX:	General Provisions
Title X:	Repeals, Redesignations, Amendments, and Other Statutes

The connection of federal aid to a particular child meant that, in theory, the aid would follow the child to any school, a point that appealed to those groups of educators, legislators, and others who had previously resisted Kennedy's proposals for federal aid to education (particularly the National Education Association and the U.S. Catholic Conference). Categorical aid helped to clear the way for the ESEA to pass through Congress (Jennings, 2000), as did the emphasis on poverty rather than race (Kaestle & Smith, 1982). Framed as compensatory education, rather than solely a focus on school desegregation, the ESEA marked a dramatic change in federal involvement in education (Kantor & Lowe, 1995). The final passage of this legislation involved the efforts of liberal reformers, interest groups and policy intellectuals, and government officials who wanted schools to subordinate to the needs of business and foreign policy (Kantor, 1991). In other words, ideology and power played a significant role in the initial ESEA legislation, and subsequent reauthorizations continue to mark changes in the federal government's involvement in public education as the policy evolves and reflects the values of respective administrations.

Of course, the Great Society and its war on poverty was short-lived, as 1965 also brought about increased U.S. involvement in the Vietnam War. Historians Harding, Kelley, and Lewis (2000) attributed the failure of the Great Society not only to costs of fighting the Vietnam War but also to other shortcomings inherent in Johnson's proposals. For one, the Job Corps and other agencies focused on job training rather than on creating new, well-paying jobs. At the same time, Johnson would not raise taxes to support these programs; instead, he stood by the tax cuts he offered to the middle class in 1964. Additionally, the war on poverty defined poverty in such a narrow way that it only included those families whose income fell below a fixed income amount (see Shannon, 1998, for explanations of how poverty is defined). Rather than engaging in efforts that would reduce income inequalities or help the poor to earn more money, the Johnson administration offered educational, legal, and job-training services, and rested on the expectation that well-paying jobs would be available to those who worked hard enough to obtain the necessary skills. This legislation reflected a widely held belief by Johnson and those who shared his liberal values that culture and behavior—not economic, social, or political forces—cause poverty. These same shortcomings from Johnson's initial legislation have remained throughout the history of subsequent reauthorizations of the ESEA: There still is a lack of well-paying jobs that no amount of job training will resolve; Congress and the president are unlikely to initiate legislation that would substantively alter the lived conditions for the middle or upper classes; and there remains a limited federal definition of poverty articulated along class lines.

Reauthorizing the Elementary and Secondary Education Act

Looking across the history of the ESEA, we can certainly see why President Johnson (1964) referred to the Great Society as "the challenge constantly renewed" (n.p.). By 1985, 20 years after the program was initiated, the ESEA was reauthorized eight times.

During the administrations of presidents Richard Nixon and Gerald Ford, the most significant change in the federal government's involvement in public education pertained to efforts to remove the federal government as much as possible from public schools (particularly financially). The Nixon administration implemented "special revenue sharing," a precursor to the Reagan administration's "block grants," as an effort to facilitate state and local decisions about education. With revenue sharing, power was given to governors, who would then decide which schools would receive money (see Jennings, 1995).

Although the federal government attempted to step away from decisions about public education, as Tyack (1991) has noted, policies often have an implementation schedule of their own, and federal influences on public schools continued from the 1960s through the 1970s. In other words, the policy changes and momentum that began in the 1960s during the Johnson administration continued into the 1970s, particularly with regard to desegregation of schools. In fact, Tyack observed that there was "far more actual racial desegregation of southern schools in the era of the rhetorical 'benign neglect' of race under President Nixon...than during the activist period preceding him that set the ideological and legal agenda of racial justice" (1991, p. 9).

When President Jimmy Carter assumed office in 1977, he faced much controversy about the federal role in public education (Dodge, Putallaz, & Malone, 2002). Some members of Congress wanted to repeal earlier legislation, to minimize or eliminate the federal involvement in and financing of public education. In spite of this, the Carter administration added billions of dollars in funding to public education (Gold, 1987) and formally established the U.S. Department of Education in 1980. President Carter assigned Shirley Hufstedler, a federal court judge, as the first Secretary of Education.

President Reagan's first reauthorization of the ESEA in 1981, the Education Consolidation Improvement Act, centralized education responsibilities with an emphasis on local control. This conservative reauthorization was a reaction to concerns about federal involvement in education and was a first effort to undo the liberal work of the 1960s and the Carter administration. In order to ensure more control by states, Reagan's reauthorization of the ESEA brought federal education programs together as block grants for states to administer; in other words, the federal government provided money toward the program, and states and local school districts were left to decide what funds would be spent and how. During this time, Title I aid (renamed Chapter I) was "reduced, and barely maintained" (McGill-Franzen, 2000, p. 891) as the conservative administration decreased federal support of public education.

George H.W. Bush's approach to education differed only slightly from that of the Reagan administration. Bush's secretary of education, William J. Bennett, attempted to secure the place of Judeo-Christian morals in public schools by endorsing particular policies such as those guaranteeing the place of constitutionally protected school prayer (see Jennings, 1995). Although the conservatism of the Reagan–Bush era generally supported the belief that the federal government should not make decisions about public education, there were exceptions to this rule when it came to espousing particular moral principles. These exceptions were due in part to the fact that the first Bush administration marked the entry of neoconservatism into federal education policy. Neoconservatism became a distinct political ideology in the 1960s when some liberals became disenchanted with enlightenment ideals that truth would "set people free." In part, they opposed the tenets of President Johnson's war on poverty, and they were disenchanted by what they considered to be a lack of morals in the counterculture and protest movements of the 1960s (Kristol, 1995). What resulted was a combination of liberal beliefs (specifically the notion that race, class, and position should not restrain individuals) and conservative concerns with order, continuity, and community (Gerson, 1996). Bush sponsored America 2000, which established national education goals (see Figure 2) that were later passed into law as the Goals 2000: Educate America Act of 1994 during the Clinton administration. (When he was governor of Arkansas, Clinton was a member of the panel that authored the goals.)

When Clinton became president of the United States, he reauthorized the ESEA as the Improving America's Schools Act of 1994. This reauthorization restated liberal values—particularly the belief that everyone can learn—with a neoliberal twist; that is, there was an explicit emphasis on capitalistic or so-called "free market" principles in all areas of

---

FIGURE 2
National Education Goals, Based on America 2000 and Declared by the Goals 2000: Educate America Act of 1994

1. School readiness—By the year 2000, all children will start school ready to learn.

2. School completion—By the year 2000, the high school graduation rate will increase to at least 90 percent.

3. Student achievement and citizenship—By the year 2000, all students will leave grades 4, 8, and 12 having demonstrated competency over challenging subject matter including English, mathematics, science, foreign languages, civics and government, economics, arts, history, and geography, and every school in America will ensure that all students learn to use their minds well, so they may be prepared for responsible citizenship, further learning, and productive employment in our Nation's modern economy.

4. Teacher education and professional development—By the year 2000, the Nation's teaching force will have access to programs for the continued improvement of their professional skills and the opportunity to acquire the knowledge and skills needed to instruct and prepare all American students for the next century.

5. Mathematics and science—By the year 2000, United States students will be first in the world in mathematics and science achievement.

6. Adult literacy and lifelong learning—By the year 2000, every adult American will be literate and will possess the knowledge and skills necessary to compete in a global economy and exercise the rights and responsibilities of citizenship.

7. Safe, disciplined, and alcohol- and drug-free schools—By the year 2000, every school in the United States will be free of drugs, violence, and the unauthorized presence of firearms and alcohol and will offer a disciplined environment conducive to learning.

8. Parental participation—By the year 2000, every school will promote partnerships that will increase parental involvement and participation in promoting the social, emotional, and academic growth of children.

From www.ed.gov/legislation/GOALS2000/TheAct/sec102.html. The objectives for each goal have not been included in the interest of space.

social, political, and business life. More specifically, the Clinton administration's education policies reflected four core neoliberal values:

1. A primacy on fostering economic growth, in this case through education that would supposedly lead to eventual success in the job market (see Street, 1995, for discussion of the myth that literacy levels will lead to employment)

2. Developing a shared sense of community that helps "them" to become more like "us"

3. Efficient educational practices modeled after business principles, including standardization and increased accountability

4. Equitable sharing of social benefits

Clinton's policies included provisions for 21st Century Community Learning Centers, bilingual education (including annual assessments and rewards for those school districts with proven success), the School-to-Work Initiative (a 1994 law that provided money for states to develop systems that focused on linking vigorous academic skills with occupations), class-size reduction, education requirements for Title I paraprofessionals, and the America Reads Challenge/Reading Excellence Act. Clinton experienced tremendous success in having his education policies pass through Congress, primarily because many of them (such as Goals 2000 and the School-to-Work Initiative) were begun during the George H.W. Bush administration (Jennings, 1995).

By the end of Clinton's second presidential term, efforts were underway again to reauthorize the ESEA as the Educational Excellence for All Children Act of 1999. This proposal continued the Clinton administration's earlier initiatives and centered around four key themes that had been emphasized in earlier legislation, including *A Nation At Risk* (National Commission on Excellence in Education, 1983), America 2000/Goals 2000, and Clinton's Call to Action for American Education. These themes were (1) setting high standards for all children; (2) improving teacher and principal quality; (3) strengthening accountability for results; and (4) ensuring safe, healthy, disciplined, and drug-free schools. However, this legislation was never authorized. Instead, George W. Bush assumed office in 2001 and proceeded to reauthorize the ESEA as the No Child Left Behind Act (although themes from the Clinton administration's proposal are evident in George W. Bush's legislation).

Signed in a low-key ceremony in an Ohio public school on January 8, 2002, No Child Left Behind is the George W. Bush administration's reauthorization of the Clinton administration's Improving America's Schools Act of 1994. No Child Left Behind includes, among other points, the following requirements:

- annual testing of students in grades 3–8 in reading and math
- adequate yearly progress to demonstrate academic improvement
- report cards that include districtwide and statewide assessment data
- highly qualified teachers and paraprofessionals
- Reading First, a new reading program for grades 1–3 that requires districts to use scientifically based reading programs
- mathematics and science partnerships linking school districts and institutions of higher education
- bilingual education programs requiring students with limited English proficiency to be tested in English after three consecutive school years in the United States
- the allowing of constitutionally protected school prayer
- access to data on 11th- and 12th-grade students for military recruitment

(For a complete list of provisions see Figure 3.)

George W. Bush's version of the ESEA has brought with it an infusion of conservative politics and neoconservative morals similar to that of the Reagan and George H.W. Bush administrations. Competitive block grants place decisions for programs such as Reading First in the hands of states, albeit with strings attached (see Edmondson & Shannon, 2003). Although the use of financial incentives to secure compliance with federal education mandates has been a mechanism in place since the Johnson administration, there has not been an administration to date that has restricted who may speak with authority about what can happen in U.S. public schools to the degree that the George W. Bush administration has. In particular, the administration's rhetoric of *scientifically based*

FIGURE 3
No Child Left Behind: Summary of Key Provisions

1. Annual testing of students in grades 3–8 in reading and math
2. Adequate yearly progress to demonstrate academic improvement
3. Report cards that include districtwide and statewide assessment data
4. Highly qualified teachers and paraprofessionals who are certified by the state in which they teach and demonstrate a high level of competence in the area they teach
5. Allocation of a portion of Title I aid for targeted grants and education finance incentives
6. Reading First, a new reading program for grades 1–3 that requires school districts to use scientifically based reading programs
7. Early Reading First, a competitive grant program intended to enhance the reading readiness of children living in high-poverty areas
8. Professional development to improve teacher and principal quality, using funds formerly allocated for class-size reduction and Eisenhower professional development
9. Mathematics and science partnerships linking school districts and institutions of higher education
10. Liability protection for educators
11. Technology, including programs and professional development for teachers in its uses
12. Bilingual education programs, requiring that students with limited English proficiency are tested in English after three consecutive school years in the United States
13. Safe and drug-free schools
14. Programs to prevent hate crimes
15. 21st Century Community Learning Centers that enhance before- and after-school initiatives to improve student learning
16. Innovative education program strategies
17. Transferability of money between major ESEA programs (with funds able to be transferred into but not out of Title I)
18. Flexibility demonstration projects, in which up to 150 districts can consolidate aid under several major ESEA programs, excluding Title I
19. Public charter schools
20. Fund for the Improvement of Education through which the secretary of education can fund educational programs
21. Rural Education with $300 million in 2002 for two programs: (1) flexible grants for small rural districts and (2) additional money for students in rural schools with a more than 20% poverty rate
22. Impact aid, which provides moneys to schools with limited tax bases
23. Information provided by the U.S. Department of Education to states, districts, and the public related to constitutionally protected school prayer, and certification by school districts that no policy prevents or denies participation in constitutionally protected prayer in public schools
24. Access to data for military recruitment
25. Use of schools for after-school Boy Scouts meetings if other outside groups are able to use the schools

Adapted from Robelon, E. (2002, January 9). An ESEA primer [Electronic version]. *Education Week, 21*(6), 28–29.

research (a term that is used 111 times in the text of the legislation [Giroux, 2003] and will be discussed in more detail in chapter 5) carries with it specific implications about who and what should direct programs in public schools. For example, G. Reid Lyon, Director of Research on Learning and Behavior at NICHD, publicly disapproved of the phonics program that the New York City public schools sought to adopt (see Goodnough, 2003a). Lyon claimed the program had no scientific evidence to prove its effectiveness, even though the author of the program explained that it was research based. The New York City schools faced losing $70 million if they adopted this program without the federal government's approval. Because of criticism from reading experts and federal and state officials, who warned that the schools could lose the federal funds, New York City school chancellor Joel I. Klein added another research-based reading program to the curriculum for the city's K–3 classrooms (Goodnough, 2003b), to be used in conjunction with the controversial phonics program. As this example shows, poor urban and rural schools, which depend on the federal government's money to help compensate for inadequate local tax bases and dramatically unequal per-pupil funding, are particularly vulnerable to the government's mandates (see Edmondson & Shannon, 2003).

Although the language and stated goals of No Child Left Behind do not differ dramatically from the aims of the Improving America's Schools Act or the national education goals (see Figure 2 on page 32), the end results of noncompliance with the federal government's stipulations and stated outcomes threaten to undo public schools throughout the United States. The rhetoric of the legislation emphasizes curriculum as a set of neutral skills to be mastered, and those who are unable or unwilling to demonstrate mastery of these skills face consequences. At the same time, the language of this legislation (i.e., "school improvement") masks a conservative agenda to privatize public schools by handing over various phases of a "school improvement" sequence to private corporations. In other words, for those schools that do not demonstrate adequate yearly progress on standardized tests (which means, for example, that by the year 2013, all students must be above the basic level in reading), a four-year school restructuring process is in order. Those schools that do not meet the stated achievement levels begin school improvement by notifying parents that the school is failing and offering them the option to send their children to another school in the district. If a school does not improve by the second year of school improvement, parents can choose to send their children for tutoring or other supplemental services at the district's expense. By the third year of school improvement, the state can intervene to make changes in curriculum and administration. If this, too, fails to raise test scores to an adequate level, by the fourth and final year of school improvement, the state can intervene to completely restructure the district. This intervention may mean subcontracting all or some of the school's duties to private corporations, as the Philadelphia, Pennsylvania, public schools did with Edison Schools Inc. (see Shannon, 2002b).

The George W. Bush administration's conservatism mixes with a neoconservative emphasis on particular (i.e., Christian) morals as members of the administration offer their suggestions for improving U.S. public education (see Smith, 2003, for further discussion of this influence). Perhaps one of the most notable examples of this Christian emphasis came in April 2003 when Secretary of Education Rod Paige (as cited in "Faith in the Public Sphere," 2003) publicly stated in an interview for Baptist Press his preference for Christian schools because of the values they teach. Specifically, he said,

> All things equal, I would prefer to have a child in a school that has a strong appreciation for the values of the Christian community, where a child is taught to have a strong faith.... In a religious environment, the value system is set.... That's not the case in a public school, where there are so many different kids with different kinds of values. (p. A24)

Criticism of Paige's statements, including calls for his resignation amid questions about the Bush administration's alliance with the religious right and its efforts to undermine public education, did not result in an apology or retraction of his statements. Instead, his statements were consistent with the Bush administration's use of public money to bolster religious and faith-based groups' involvement in prisons, substance abuse programs, housing construction, and other areas (see "Faith," 2003; Sorel & Lingeman, 2003). Former Secretary of Education Bennett defended Paige and supported his statements, insisting that "values that were born of or nurtured by the Christian faith—form a strong basis for good citizenship in school and beyond. Public schools would do well to teach them" (Bennett, 2003, p. B07).

As federal policy has influenced schools and local communities, groups have come together to respond to and resist these changes, particularly around the issue of high-stakes standardized testing. Organizations such as FairTest (www.fairtest.org) and publications from Rethinking Schools (www.rethinkingschools.org) work through coalitions and grassroots efforts to educate parents and the general public concerning policy issues and the effects that policy has on local schools and communities, and to mobilize for change. These efforts reflect radical democratic commitment to social equity and change that includes the conditions for a participatory democracy that values the voices of those who often are silenced and excluded in U.S. society and U.S. public schools.

Policy Lessons: Implications for Teachers

Teachers are not the only group paying attention to education policy, particularly to George W. Bush's No Child Left Behind Act. Newspaper journalists and commentators throughout the United States and the world have noticed as well. From *The Boston Globe* and *The Washington Post* to *The Irish Times* and Malaysia's *New Straits Times*, writers have variously pondered, critiqued, and/or endorsed key aspects of the act. School choice, mandatory standardized testing, military recruitment linked to federal school funding, and other topics arise throughout these stories as writers describe the contradictions, concerns, and hopes the policy represents. It seems that no other educational policy, at least none in recent history, has generated more discussion, debate, or attention. At the same time, never before have more federal dollars been spent on public education, and never before has the federal government been more prescriptive about how that money should be spent.

The following list provides options for the ways in which teachers can begin to critically engage in policy study:

1. Recognize the values inherent in any given policy. From this brief explanation of the history of the ESEA, the most important lesson is that policy is always influenced by someone's values. In this short history, we see the various values and influences of federal visions for U.S. public schools and, ultimately, society. From conservative values for local control to neoliberal calls to secure the United States's place of power within the global economy, there are confluences of values, visions, compromises, and debates in the different iterations of this legislation.

We have yet to consider how this policy articulates at different levels of implementation—in states, in local districts, and in classrooms—as teachers and school officials exercise power and influence over the particulars of this policy. We will turn to these issues and continued discussion of political values in the next chapters.

2. Attend to the contradictions in policies. Another lesson is that policies, like any human endeavors, are riddled with contradictions. Attention to these contradictions is the best starting point for change. For example, foremost in Johnson's liberal vision for a Great Society was a war on poverty, which was supposed to be waged by affluent people in an affluent culture (Marcuse, 2001). Public education was to assume the front line in this war, and it has continued to largely be viewed as the "place where Americans seek to transform the ideology of the American dream into practice" (Hochschild, 2001, p. 35). However, will such a policy ever bring significant social change that disrupts the status quo, particularly if responsibility for this change is placed primarily in the hands of those who are best served by the status quo? Are there other ways to address much-needed questions of equity in U.S. public schools? Are there other groups that should be involved? Considering this contradiction should open up questions, of which the previous ones are just a few, that allow us to consider different possibilities about poverty and U.S. public education.

3. Expect education policy to bring change. Finally, we learn that policy can and does bring changes to schools, some that may not occur otherwise. For example, the teachers in Heath's (1983) study may not have engaged in inquiries about language and culture had they not been pressed upon to do so because of the ESEA and the Civil Rights movement's desegregation requirements, and without these influences they may not have engaged in the changes in their instruction that were responsive to their students' communities. Policies can bring changes that are beneficial, or they can bring changes that we expect will do harm. It is up to us as educators to influence policy in directions that are constructive, rather than closing our doors and hoping policy will go away.

In the chapters that follow, we will turn to three educators and their efforts to do just this: influence policy in directions they choose. First will be the story of a fourth-grade teacher who believed children should be given time to read silently as part of reading instruction in his classroom.

CHAPTER 3

The Chain Gang:
Sustained Silent Reading
in Scientific Times

CRITICAL POLICY STUDY QUESTIONS ADDRESSED

Who are the policymakers?

What are the values of the policymakers?

Why was the policy initiated?

In Dan Roberts's fourth-grade classroom in Pennsylvania, a paper chain made its way around the ceiling's perimeter. "We're going to try to make it around the room at least once," Mr. Roberts commented as we visited together after school on a cold January day. Each of the nearly 200 links in the paper chain contained the title and author of a book a child in his class had completed during silent reading time, and each link was signed proudly by the child in his or her best fourth-grade handwriting. As I glanced at the chain, I could see links that read "*Where the Red Fern Grows* (Wilson Rawls)," "*Poppy and Rye* (Avi)," "*Tales of a Fourth Grade Nothing* (Judy Blume)," "*The Gadget* (Paul Zindel)," and "*Harry Potter and the Goblet of Fire* (J.K. Rowling)." It seemed like impressive reading for a group of 9- and 10-year-olds, but then again, as Mr. Roberts explained, this was a class of readers. These children read on their way to the cafeteria. They read on their way to physical education class. They read on the playground. They even named themselves "The Bookworms," a title that proudly capped the newsletters they wrote for parents each month.

When I asked Mr. Roberts why he decided to make the paper chain, he replied,

> Because I feel, especially this year for the first time, that silent reading may be on its way out, that the idea of dropping everything and just reading is sort of becoming a thing of the past. And I don't want that. I don't want to see it happen. So if I can show the principal and the other teachers how important it is to the kids, and how much we accomplish in doing it, then I think it says something. (personal communication, January 16, 2003)

Test scores in Mr. Roberts's school district, while still well above the state average, were lower than the district average in his particular school. Because of this, the administration told teachers to spend more time teaching specific reading strategies and suggested that any reading time should be conducted with instructional books used in reading groups. If this policy were followed, the time that children curled up with books of their choice and indulged in the pleasure of reading would no longer be considered reading instruction.

Mr. Roberts did not disagree with his administration's suggestion that reading instruction should teach reading strategies, nor did he disagree that children should explicitly be taught specifics about the content and processes of reading. In fact, he was actively trying to improve his own teaching of reading by enrolling in optional professional development courses on reading strategy instruction. He continually sought out information from researchers and educators such as Janet Allen, Regie Routman, Stephanie Harvey, and Sharon Taberski, along with reports such as that of the National Reading Panel (NICHD, 2000). So while Mr. Roberts agreed that children needed to learn reading strategies, he took issue with the suggestion that time should be taken away from children to enjoy reading books of their choice.

Mr. Roberts's situation is not unique. Other teachers are similarly scratching their heads about recommendations to eliminate silent reading (see Edmondson & Shannon, 2002, for one example). Although the government-commissioned report *Becoming a Nation of Readers: The Report of the Commission on Reading* (Anderson et al., 1985) strongly urged educators to engage students in silent reading by stating "Children of every age and ability ought to be doing more extended silent reading" (p. 54), times have changed. More than a decade after

Becoming a Nation of Readers was released, the National Research Council's report *Preventing Reading Difficulties in Young Children* (Snow, Burns, & Griffin, 1998) issued recommendations encouraging teachers to allow time for children to read on their own, but with some subtle caveats attached. The report added the stipulation that children should be carefully matched with texts that were of interest to and readable by the child. To do so would require a degree of monitoring and intervention by the child's teacher or another knowledgeable adult. Specifically, the report stated that, in the early grades

> time, materials, and resources should be provided...to support daily independent reading of texts selected to be of particular interest for the individual student, and beneath the individual student's frustration level, in order to consolidate the student's capacity for independent reading. (p. 8)

Just two years later, the release of the National Reading Panel's report (NICHD, 2000) began the trend of casting silent reading as irrelevant to reading instruction, making it an artifact of the past in many U.S. public schools:

> It would be difficult to interpret this collection of studies [of sustained silent reading] as representing clear evidence that encouraging students to read more actually improves reading achievement.... [G]iven the evidence that exists, the Panel cannot conclude that schools should adopt programs to encourage more reading if the intended goal is to improve reading achievement.... There are few beliefs more widely held than that teachers should encourage students to engage in voluntary reading and that if they did this successfully, better reading achievement would result. Unfortunately, research has not clearly demonstrated this relationship. In fact the handful of experimental studies in which this idea has been tried raises serious questions about the efficacy of some of these procedures. (pp. 3-26–3-27)

So why this apparent change in "official policy"? Who constituted this National Reading Panel, and whose values are represented in these governmental decisions? These are questions to explore in more detail as we attempt to answer Mr. Roberts's critical policy study questions concerning why such a policy was initiated and by whom.

Who Are the Policymakers?
Members of the National Reading Panel

By the end of their first meeting, the National Reading Panel's work was divided into subgroups that drew in part on *Preventing Reading Difficulties in Young Children* (Snow et al., 1998). These groups represented areas of expertise for many of the Panel members (see Table 3 for a summary of Panel members' biographies and publications; full publication information can be found in the reference list). Linnea C. Ehri led the group on alphabetics, a primary focus of her research before becoming a Panel member, and she worked on her subcommittee with Dale M. Willows, a scholar in reading development and reading difficulties. Michael L. Kamil led the comprehension and technology group, his area of expertise. Timothy Shanahan, who is interested in research synthesis in reading, as well as policy issues (personal communication, May 2, 2001), cochaired the methods groups with Sally Shaywitz, a pediatrician with expertise in medical research and who was a member of the National Research Council for the *Preventing Reading Difficulties in Young Children* (Snow et al., 1998) report. S. Jay Samuels helped to lead the fluency group. Thomas Trabasso conducted comprehension research and was a member of the comprehension subcommittee. Joanna Williams conducted research that focused on reading comprehension with disabled readers. Other Panel members included Gloria Correro, a professor and associate dean from Mississippi State University; Cora Bagley Marrett, Vice Chancellor for Academic Affairs and Provost at the University of Massachusetts–Amherst; Donald Langenberg, a physicist and Chancellor of the 13-member University of Maryland System; Gwenette Ferguson, a reading teacher; Joanne Yatvin, a school administrator; and Norma Garza, a certified public accountant and parent.

According to Yatvin (as cited in Allington, 2002), there were noted distinctions on the Panel between those who were considered "experts" and those who were not:

> All the scientist members held the same general view of the reading process. With no powerful voices from other philosophical camps on the panel, it was easy for this majority to believe that theirs was the only legitimate view. (p. 128)

TABLE 3

Biographies of National Reading Panel members

Panel Member	Position at the Time of National Reading Panel Work	Areas of Expertise and Recognition (based on published research and work experience)	Sample Publications Relevant to Panel Work
Gloria Correro	Professor and Associate Dean, Mississippi State University	Founder of kindergarten and early childhood programs in Mississippi	
Linnea C. Ehri	Distinguished Professor of Educational Psychology, Graduate School and University Center of the City University of New York	Researcher of early reading development and instruction	Beginning reading from a psycholinguistic perspective: Amalgamation of word identities. (Ehri, 1978) Learning to read and spell words. (Ehri, 1987) Grapheme-phoneme knowledge is essential for learning to read words in English. (Ehri, 1998) Pictorial mnemonics for phonics. (Ehri, Deffner, & Wilce, 1984)
Gwenette Ferguson	Reading teacher from Houston, Texas	Recipient of Kirby Middle School Award for Outstanding Dedication and Service, and Houston Area Alliance of Black School Educators Outstanding Educator Award, among others	
Norma Garza	Certified public accountant from Brownsville, Texas	Founder and chair of the Brownsville Reads Task Force; member of the Governor's Focus on Reading Task Force, Governor's Special Education Advisory Committee, and Texas panel of Academics Goals 2000	

Panel Member	Position at the Time of National Reading Panel Work	Areas of Expertise and Recognition (based on published research and work experience)	Sample Publications Relevant to Panel Work
Michael L. Kamil	Professor of Psychological Studies in Education and Learning, Design, and Technology, School of Education, Stanford University, Stanford, California	Chair of Technology Committee of National Reading Conference; former editor of *Journal of Reading Behavior*; coeditor of Volumes I, II, and III of *Handbook of Reading Research*	Quantitative trends in publication of research on technology and reading, writing, and literacy. (Kamil & Intrator, 1998) Effects of other technologies on literacy and literacy learning. (Kamil, Intrator, & Kim, 2000) Researching the relation between technology and literacy: An agenda for the 21st century. (Kamil & Lane, 1998) Models of the reading process. (Samuels & Kamil, 1984)
Donald Langenberg	Eminent physicist and Chancellor of the 13-member University System of Maryland	Former Chancellor of the University of Illinois at Chicago, Deputy Director (and Acting Director) of National Science Foundation, and Professor of Physics at the University of Pennsylvania	
Cora Bagley Marrett	Vice Chancellor for Academic Affairs and Provost at the University of Massachusetts–Amherst	Former Assistant Director of National Science Foundation (1992–1996), who first led the Directorate for Social, Behavioral and Economic Sciences; former Director of the United Negro College Fund/Mellon Programs	

(continued)

T A B L E 3 (c o n t i n u e d)
Biographies of National Reading Panel members

Panel Member	Position at the Time of National Reading Panel Work	Areas of Expertise and Recognition (based on published research and work experience)	Sample Publications Relevant to Panel Work
S. Jay Samuels	Professor, Department of Educational Psychology, University of Minnesota	Reading researcher, consultant to inner-city schools, member of Reading Hall of Fame, and recipient of other distinguished awards for reading research	The method of repeated readings. (Samuels, 1979) Units of word recognition: Evidence for developmental changes. (Samuels, LaBerge, & Bremer, 1978) Practice effects on the unit of word recognition. (Samuels, Miller, & Eisenberg, 1979)
Timothy Shanahan	Professor of Urban Education, Director of the Center for Literacy, and Coordinator of Graduate Programs in Reading, Writing and Literacy, University of Illinois at Chicago	Reading researcher with extensive experience with children in Head Starr, children with special needs, and children in inner-city schools	Assumptions underlying educational intervention research: A commentary on Harris and Pressley. (Shanahan, 1994) Reading-writing relationships, thematic units, inquiry learning…In pursuit of effective integrated literacy instruction. (Shanahan, 1997) Literacy research that makes a difference. (Shanahan & Neuman, 1997)
Sally Shaywitz	Professor of Pediatrics and Co-Director, Yale Center for the Study of Learning and Attention, Yale University School of Medicine, New Haven, Connecticut	Neuroscientist noted for contributions in reading development and reading disorders, including recent demonstration of neurobiological substrate of reading and reading disability	Cognitive profiles of reading disability: Comparisons of discrepancy and low achievement definitions. (Fletcher et al., 1994) The case for early reading intervention. (Foorman, Francis, Shaywitz, Shaywitz, & Fletcher, 1997) Developmental lag versus deficit models of reading disability: A longitudinal, individual grown curves analysis. (Francis, Shaywitz, Stuebing, Shaywitz, & Fletcher, 1996)

Panel Member	Position at the Time of National Reading Panel Work	Areas of Expertise and Recognition (based on published research and work experience)	Sample Publications Relevant to Panel Work
Thomas Trabasso	Irving B. Harris Professor, Department of Psychology, The University of Chicago	Cognitive scientist who investigated comprehension during reading and developed connectionist model that simulates dynamic processing over the course of reading	Strategic processing during comprehension. (Magliano, Trabasso, & Graesser, 1999)
Joanna Williams	Professor of Psychology and Education, Columbia University, New York	Researcher of linguistic, cognitive, and perceptual bases of reading development and disorders; member of the Reading Hall of Fame and recipient of other distinguished awards for reading research	Comprehension of students with and without learning disabilities: Identification of narrative themes and idiosyncratic text representations. (Williams, 1993) Improving the comprehension of disabled readers. (Williams, 1998) An instructional program in comprehension of narrative themes for adolescents with learning disabilities. (Williams, Brown, & Silverstein, 1994)
Dale M. Willows	Professor, Department of Human Development and Applied Psychology, Ontario Institute for Studies in Education, Toronto, Ontario, Canada	Scholar in reading development and reading difficulties	Reading ability and text difficulty as influences on second graders' oral reading errors. (Blaxall & Willows, 1984) Information-processing patterns in specific reading disability. (Watson & Willows, 1995) The development of grammatical sensitivity and its relationship to early reading achievement. (Willows & Ryan, 1986)
Joanne Yatvin	Principal of Cottrell and Bull Run Schools, Boring, Oregon	Classroom teacher and school administrator with 41 years' experience	

Adapted from www.nationalreadingpanel.org/NRPAbout/Biographies.htm.

In order for us to make sense of the Panel's recommendations and the implications for teachers like Mr. Roberts, it seems necessary to understand what the view held by these scientists might be.

To organizations such as the National Institutes of Health, it was standard practice to assemble committees because of expertise, as Alexandra Wigdor from the National Academy of Sciences and the National Research Council explained during the first full Panel meeting:

> Members of our committees are selected for their expertise, period.... That is the first criterion. Given that we then select members to try to have a rich and valuable representation of age, region, ethnicity, and obviously the various scientists that need to be there but the primary criterion is always expertise. Members do not sit on our committee as representative of any group or any community of interests, or any policy position and, indeed, we make a rather big deal at the beginning of the committee process of making sure that the committee members understand that they have to leave their political enthusiasms at the door. (National Reading Panel, 1998a, p. 12, lines 5–16)

While assembling an expert panel seems at some level to be a reasonable move, particularly given the limited time allocated for the Panel's work, questions can and should be raised concerning why those who assembled the National Reading Panel did not seek to bring together a more diverse expert group. There were no sociologists, anthropologists, or historians among the group, to name a few possible alternatives. Because achieving consensus was a primary goal from the outset of the Panel's work (see National Reading Panel, 1998a), it is more easily attainable with like-minded individuals who shared similar values. Perhaps the most notable shared value across the National Reading Panel pertained to science and the use of science to determine the best methods for teaching reading. In what follows, we consider in more detail the values of the National Reading Panel, what scientific research is, and what its limitations are.

Values of the National Reading Panel

Around the time that Mr. Roberts was beginning his teaching career, Panel members were beginning their meetings. There was little dissent among the group members about what should be done; that is, they interpreted the Congressional charge to be a call for reviewing the scientific studies of reading. Although a series of regional meetings were held between May and July of 1998, potentially allowing for different viewpoints to be expressed (National Reading Panel, 1998a), there is little evidence that these meetings influenced the Panel's decisions and course of action. In fact, any hope a Panel member may have had about incorporating a recommendation from the regional meetings into their work was discouraged, as Duane Alexander from NICHD explained to the Panel:

> And in fact, it would be nice to be able to do something about many of these [requests from the regional meetings] in the report, and address these people's concerns, but it is not in the charge. And if we try to do all these things, we will neglect the charge that is before us, that the Congress asked us to do. And we have to focus our efforts just on the charge, which is more than enough work for us to do already. If you look at the charge from the Congress, really the key term is "assess the status of research-based knowledge." (National Reading Panel, 1998b, p. 6, lines 8–15)

Scientific, experimental research was perhaps the most apparent value held collectively by the National Reading Panel membership. If any Panel member doubted that their focus should be directed toward science, they were reassured early in the Panel's meetings to proceed in this direction. Alexander emphasized Congress' intent for

> high scientific quality standards [to] be used by this panel in doing its work…there is a sense of frustration and some anger that higher standards have not been applied in evaluating research results in this field before programs were built on them, and [there is] the expectation that this Panel will set a course toward rectifying that situation. (National Reading Panel, 1998b, p. 7, lines 8–16)

This point did concern some Panel members, but only to the extent that they anticipated criticism from their peers for this focus. For example, during a discussion about the methodology the subgroups were following, Kamil stated,

> What I am worried about is what our colleagues in reading research are going to look at and what they are going to say about what we are doing. We have left out so much and concentrated on so little that what would

worry me is to start talking about overarching principles.... The overarching principles are exactly what are upsetting our colleagues who do not believe in experimental work in the same way we do...the experimental literature is a small part of [the work in journals] and it is increasingly becoming smaller. That does not mean that it is good or bad. It means that we have got a field that we have to address that has different assumptions from what we have. (National Reading Panel, 1999b, p. 24, lines 1–21)

No one on the Panel overtly disagreed with his statement. Although there was recognition that others in reading research and literacy education valued different ways of knowing, the Panel exclusively searched out experimental research. Their attention was turned toward randomized, clinical research in each subgroup area, and although they debated the merits of particular experimental reports of research (including research design and the significance of findings), they largely agreed about what was acceptable for their review (a more thorough discussion of experimental research appears in the following section).

Because of this focus, when the National Reading Panel's efforts turned to research on silent reading—Mr. Roberts's concern—there was no "gold-standard" scientific evidence (i.e., experimental research) to support it (see Coles, 2003, for a critique of the Panel's handling of the research on silent reading). Shanahan reviewed the literature on silent reading. As he presented his case to the other Panel members, he first discussed the popularity of silent reading and the correlational studies showing that children who read a lot tended to be better readers (National Reading Panel, 1999a, p. 273). He noted the popular promotion of silent reading in teacher education programs and textbooks, and then concluded,

My sense of the overall literature on SSR is, indeed, it does not work but my sense of the studies that have managed to meet our criteria is not that we even have enough to look at SSR. What we have enough to say is that there are not many studies in this area, that there are not very many good studies, well done studies in this area, and that we really do not feel that there is any possibility of concluding that these procedures work or that they do not work from evidence that exists. That is the—to me that is the cautious and appropriate level of response. (National Reading Panel, 1999a, p. 311, lines 20–22; p. 312, lines 1–9)

After the report was released, Shanahan's position was questioned by Krashen (2000) in *Education Week*, and by other researchers and educators in other venues (see Coles 2003; Cunningham, 2001; Garan, 2002). These critiques focused most directly on the Panel's interpretation, or misinterpretation, of the existing research on silent reading, and on the "good" or "bad" science engaged in studies of the effects of extended and uninterrupted time for reading books.

The definitions and logic of scientifically based research are important to understand, particularly given the priority that scientifically based research has attained in reading policies from the Reading Excellence Act of 1998 to the present. Although this emphasis has been welcomed by some (see NICHD, 2000), it has occurred amid controversy and debate (Lagemann, 2000; Shavelson & Towne, 2002).

A Scientific Definition of Reading and Research

Over the past decade, like no other time in the past, control over what it means to read and to teach reading has been articulated in federal policy. Former president Clinton defined reading as the ability to read a book independently by the end of the third grade. Congress likewise proposed a definition focusing primarily on skills (see the Reading Excellence Act definition in the glossary, page 12). At the same time, Congress explicitly named the need for reading to be taught using principles based on reliable, replicable research. The National Reading Panel took this advice seriously and proposed that reading research could be useful only if it adhered to scientifically based procedures. What resulted was a definition of reading that focused on five areas: (1) phonemic awareness, (2) phonics, (3) fluency, (4) vocabulary, and (5) comprehension. This definition is consistent with the recommendations offered in *Preventing Reading Difficulties in Young Children* (Snow et al., 1998), along with other definitions of reading that engage technical aspects of literacy. Studies that strive for scientific standards require by design a particular and arguably specific definition of reading. In other words, for reading to be measurable in the ways that scientific studies require, the act of reading becomes what Street (1995) refers to as "autonomous," necessitating a focus on reading as a neutral and technical skill that can be broken into incremental parts, taught, and tested.

On February 6, 2002, during a Department of Education symposium on the uses of scientifically based research in education, researchers and government officials described definitions and assumptions of scientific research in education. To the U.S. Department of Education and the Office of Educational Research and Improvement (OERI), the best scientific research is empirical (in other words, it can be observed) and is based on objective evidence (Reyna, 2002). In general, the experts speaking at this symposium pointed to three types of research: (1) experimental, (2) quasi-experimental, and (3) translational. Each are briefly described in what follows and summarized in Table 4.

The goals of scientifically based experimental research include the hope of generalizing findings and interventions to a large group of people (Reyna, 2002). For such possibilities to exist, according to scientific research principles, the "best evidence" for generating scientific knowledge involves research that has a control group and an experimental group. This means that children—who for the purposes of the research design are considered to be essentially the same as far as age, abilities, race, class, and gender—would be randomly assigned to one or more groups. Then, they would be compared on reading tasks specific to the

TABLE 4	
Summary of Primary Scientific Research Designs	
Types of Scientific Research	Description
Experimental	• Random assignment (or approximation of random assignment) of subjects to control or experimental group • Testing of cause–effect relations
Quasi-experimental	• Statistical manipulation of groups when random assignment is not possible • Sometimes used because of ethical concerns about control groups
Translational	• Application of established theory to classroom practice • Involves scientific inquiry—hypothesizing outcome and then testing to validate hypothesis

research question after the experimental group received a "treatment" (for example, a particular method of instruction) and the control group did not. This research is sometimes referred to as the "gold standard" for scientific research because it is considered to offer the highest level of evidence that a particular intervention works or does not work. Such research assumes that it is possible to obtain a random sample (or at least approximate one). It also assumes that the experimental and control groups are equivalent at the beginning of the research project so that any measured change between the groups is directly attributable to the treatment.

When this gold-standard experimental research is not possible, the Department of Education has suggested the use of quasi-experimental research. This research type involves using "statistical magic [where the researcher can] artificially create a sort of comparison or control by sort of equating people on things" (Reyna, 2002, p. 10). It allows researchers to study the hypothesized *cause* of differences in research findings between groups after the findings have already occurred (see Salkind, 2000). For example, a researcher hypothesizing about the cause of differences in reading achievement between fourth-grade students who attend a public school and those who are home schooled cannot randomly assign individuals to groups. The groups are already established. For this reason, a different approach to the research is required if it is going to be quasi-experimental.

Another use of quasi-experimental designs is when a researcher cannot assign individuals to a control group because of ethical concerns or another reason. A quasi-experimental research design allows the researcher to account for nonrandomization of assignment to experimental or control groups through statistical manipulations of the data. Quasi-experimental research is not considered to have the same degree of power to predict as experimental designs does (Salkind, 2000).

A third scientific way of knowing described by the Department of Education is translational research. This research type involves the extrapolation of evidence-based theories to classroom use (see Reyna, 2002). Evidence-based theories have been confirmed or disconfirmed through scientific study and then appropriated for classroom use. In other words, researchers consider a theory about how someone learns, and then they generalize it to a classroom situation. The generalization of theory involves hypothesizing about a particular outcome before beginning the study (an approach that is different from the inductive methods employed in qualitative research) and then testing results to see if the outcome was achieved.

The U.S. Department of Education endorsed the position that evaluation of scientific research should be based not only on the method employed but also on the relevance and significance of the study (Reyna, 2002). Human values and decision making affect such decisions. One official from the Center for Education at the National Research Council explained,

> Science is intendedly rational, it is disciplined, it is honest, it is open, we aspire to a kind of dispassionate, politically neutral distillation of evidence to make decisions.... At the same time, I want to tell you that what scientists themselves often acknowledge is that there is a dimension of human judgment that can be missed with an overzealous focus on the rigors of scientific method. (Feuer, 2002, p. 21)

So although the intention of science may be rationality and neutrality, it is decidedly human and subjective at the same time (see Smith, 2003). As scientists strive to safeguard their methodologies and procedures in order to maintain objectivity, they factor out (i.e., ignore) the social and cultural issues that complicate literacy teaching and learning. Trabasso made this quite clear during the second meeting of the National Reading Panel when he pointed out the following:

> I think it is impossible to be quote "objective" unquote. You are going to have—you always have some.... Everything is interpreted, okay? Everything is constructed. The question is whether or not we get some degree of support independently of our own opinions. That is what we are looking for. (National Reading Panel, 1998b, p. 120, lines 25–30)

During the Department of Education symposium, one speaker from OERI asked what the alternatives to scientifically based research might be. This question is important; yet it was not treated particularly seriously. The speaker only named anecdote, tradition, and superstition as possible alternatives. What she failed to name were other ways of knowing, which might include historical, cultural, anthropological, sociological, moral, and ethical understandings. As a group, reading educators have learned much about literacy, language, and teaching from research studies that do not meet the gold-standard scientific criteria previously outlined. We have learned a considerable amount through ethnographic, observational, and other interpretive studies, including the books and research to which Mr. Roberts has turned as he has attempted to improve his own teaching. Heath (1983) taught us that the learning and use of language and literacy are cultural, and she reminded educators of the importance of bridging home and school discourses. Cambourne (2000) has observed conditions that foster literacy learning that include many implications for classroom organization and practice. Shannon (1998) has taught us about the political and economic aspects of literacy as well as how to read poverty. Delpit (1995) has helped us to consider how process approaches to writing and student-centered instruction might not benefit young African American children. Finders (1997) points out the complexities of the literacies that junior high school girls use both in and out of school, and how these girls' literacies differ across economic class boundaries. Brandt (2001) has noted the accumulating effects of literacy across generations, reminding us of the ways in which people come to change literacy (even if institutions do not change the way it is taught). Powell (1999) has taught us about the moral imperative of literacy. There are many more such studies that space does not allow me to name, but the point should be clear. As Kamil noted to the National Reading Panel, much research in reading exists that draws on disciplines and methods other than empirical science. These alternatives are research studies that reflect more than anecdote, tradition, and superstition, and while they may not follow the scientific standards endorsed by the U.S. federal government, they have contributed and will continue to contribute significantly to our understandings of literacy and our teaching of reading in U.S. public schools.

Those researchers who endorse scientifically based reading research studies as the primary source of information for U.S. public schools suggest that to do otherwise is dangerous and morally reprehensible (Reyna, 2002). However, it also has been argued that to ignore the social and ideological aspects of literacy instruction is equally dangerous and reprehensible, if not more so (see Heath, 1983, for one discussion of the dangers of not attending to social and ideological aspects of literacy). Instead of working to narrow the type of research that is conducted in education contexts, public policy in education should focus on guaranteeing Fourteenth Amendment rights. As such, it seems that generation of knowledge through a variety of research methods, approaches, and epistemological bases, of which science is but one possibility, should be valued and protected by education policy.

Policy Lessons: Implications for Teachers

Mr. Roberts's experiences with the policy on silent reading and his administrator's corresponding expectation for scientific research point to at least two lessons on effecting policy change:

1. Trust your experience and your knowledge. Mr. Roberts's personal classroom policy is not based on science or formal experimental studies. Instead, his stand on silent reading as valuable reading instruction is based on his own experience, filtered through his study of pedagogy and literacy learning. As he explained,

> My 11th-grade English teacher was the one. It took me until 11th grade before I started to love to read, and he was the one who said, "I have this wonderful book." He had books and books and books all over the room, and he said, "I don't care what you choose. Choose any book you want." He said, "You're going to read it, and you're going to write to me in this dialogue journal. We're going to write to each other." And it was the first time a teacher ever said, "You choose." I picked the smallest book I could find, which was *The Old Man and the Sea*, [by] Ernest Hemingway, and I fell in love with it. Lucky choice, right? (personal communication, January 16, 2003)

From this time on, Mr. Roberts explained, he became an avid reader, particularly of children's books. He saw the value of offering students the choice and the time to read, aspects of reading instruction that have been validated by reading researchers such as Routman (1988).

2. Work locally, beginning in your own classrooms and schools. Mr. Roberts's silent protest is a lesson in working locally to begin to effect policy change. As other teachers in Mr. Roberts's building noticed the paper chain in his classroom, he taught them about the threat to silent reading and his concerns about the school district's new reading instruction policy. Another fourth-grade teacher began the same protest, an act of solidarity with Mr. Roberts and an expression of hope to retain silent reading in her classroom as well. One fifth-grade teacher began to seriously question the new reading instruction policy and to think about the opportunities during the school day when her students would have the choice and the time to read.

Mr. Roberts's protest of his school district's new reading instruction policy also taught children that spending time reading is important, even if not everyone values it. He kept children at the center of his efforts, even though legislative and policy discussions about reading seemed to lose sight of them. Through his protest, he was teaching children that they could make decisions about their own reading and that it was important to set aside time for engagement with texts. Mr. Roberts explained,

> I really try to step back and look at the big picture because you can get so tied down looking at this standard or this objective that I have to meet, and [whether] all my kids know how to create a web on a computer. And when I think about that, I wonder how important is it really for them to be able to do that this year, right now, as opposed to whether I developed or nurtured a love of reading and writing in these kids...if they can come back 10 years from now and say, "You know, you opened my eyes to books. I had a great year in fourth grade," then I've done something. You know if I didn't teach them how to spell every word correctly, that's OK. If they started to like reading books, if [author] Gary Paulsen hooked those boys who hated books coming in, I think I've done my job. (personal communication, January 16, 2003)

In addition to teaching teachers and children, Mr. Roberts's paper chain informed parents, perhaps the most important ally in effecting local policy change. As parents entered his classroom, Mr. Roberts had the opportunity to explain the paper chain to them. Providing parents with accurate information on reading and policy can help them to understand current trends and issues, and it can encourage parents' political participation in decisions about schools. The information that teachers provide to parents about teaching and learning can inform parents' conversations with administrators and specialists within the school district. At the same time, this information also will help parents to make knowledgeable decisions when voting for school board members and local and state representatives, to work politically through groups such as the Parent Teacher Association (PTA), and to do much more. The reciprocal learning and teaching relationship that can occur between parents and teachers is powerful in effecting change (see

Goodman, 2001, as well as www.FairTest.org, for ideas about the potential for parent-teacher collaborations).

If district policy continued to discourage silent reading time at the beginning of the next school year, Mr. Roberts planned to make a new paper chain with his new class, and he expected that he would discuss the paper chain during his Back to School Night in the fall. He planned to continue to explain the importance of silent reading time to other teachers and administrators, and he hoped to continue to foster a love of reading among his students by making time in their busy days to enjoy uninterrupted time with books. The same experience made him a reader, along with countless other children who have been students in his class.

From Mr. Roberts we learn that we can trust our experiences when we are thoughtfully engaged in teaching children. Mr. Roberts understood what was best for his students, and he checked this experience against his reading of professional literature. He read broadly, not limiting himself to one perspective or position, and he weighed these readings against what he understood children in his classroom would need.

From Mr. Roberts, we also learn that policies have local iterations. These iterations are in teachers' control, and this is where policy can most immediately be changed. Mr. Roberts's use of the paper chain in his classroom was a way to show the problems with the silent reading policy, and it became a venue for expressing his concerns about this policy to his administrators, his fellow teachers, and his students' parents. In addition to these groups, he could have invited local school board members and legislators to his classroom to see his work. These two groups can do much to understand and be responsive to local policy issues.

CHAPTER 4

Working for a Schooling: The Consequences of Business Models in Students' and Teachers' Lives

CRITICAL POLICY STUDY QUESTION ADDRESSED

What are the consequences of the policy?

Rob Charleson worked for two years as a schoolteacher in a Detroit, Michigan, USA, area public charter school. In this position, he and a coteacher educated 50 students in a combined fourth- and fifth-grade classroom. The students primarily came from lower class and working class communities outside Detroit. During the time that Mr. Charleson taught in this school, the school choice movement and the emphasis on accountability through standards and high-stakes testing were particularly influential. By the end of the 1990s, public charter schools were offering parents and students school "choice" by providing alternatives to regular public schools. According to www.uscharter schools.org (US Charter Schools, 2003), an online community developed in conjunction with the U.S. Department of Education, charter schools are

> nonsectarian public schools of choice that operate with freedom from
> many of the regulations that apply to traditional public schools. The
> "charter" establishing each such school is a performance contract detailing
> the school's mission, program, goals, students served, methods of assess-
> ment, and ways to measure success. The length of time for which charters

are granted varies, but most are granted for 3–5 years. At the end of the term, the entity granting the charter may renew the school's contract. Charter schools are accountable to their sponsor—usually a state or local school board—to produce positive academic results and adhere to the charter contract. The basic concept of charter schools is that they exercise increased autonomy in return for this accountability. They are accountable for both academic results and fiscal practices to several groups: the sponsor that grants them, the parents who choose them, and the public that funds them.

Former president Clinton first proposed a public charter school program in 1993, generating federal interest among the members of Congress. When the ESEA was reauthorized as the Improving America's Schools Act of 1994, the public charter school program became incorporated into Title X, Part C, with an initial appropriation of $6 million (see www.uscharterschools.org). In 1998, Congress passed the Charter School Expansion Act, committing $145 million to this initiative.

During this same time period, neoliberal rhetoric became prevalent, casting children as "human capital" and schools as training grounds for future employment in a globalized economy (see Smith & Scoll, 1995). Clinton administration policies reflecting this trend included America Reads, which forwarded the tenet that all children should learn to read well and independently by the end of the third grade in order to have success in school and later the job market (see Edmondson, 2000), as well as the School-to-Work initiative, which provided money to schools and communities that competed to bring the initiative to their area (see Shannon, 2002a). Mr. Charleson's school was no exception to this trend. In his charter school, there was a business management system in place to help improve efficiency and productivity in the school, as well as a Job Corps program requiring students to work for "school money." Mr. Charleson was not particularly enamored with these influences, and his uncertainty about them led him to engage in critical policy study that unraveled the rhetoric and values implicit in these policies.

To understand the consequences that neoliberal language (manifest in business models for schooling) brings to public education, particularly as it limits full participation in decisions about education, we need to take a closer look at the ways in which business influences are realized in U.S. public schools. Critical policy study can help to unravel the language and ideology of neoliberal education policy. To begin, we will consider an explanation of the business model operating at Mr. Charleson's school, along with Mr. Charleson's questions about the consequences such policies hold for children and teachers in U.S. public schools.

The Business of Education

Education at Mr. Charleson's school was guided by the Baldrige Systems Management business philosophy. Malcolm Baldrige, Secretary of Commerce during the Reagan administration, first developed his criteria for business in the 1970s. His approach was formulated in response to concerns about manufacturing quality in U.S. businesses, and he sought innovations to improve production and efficiency in U.S. industry.

Benchmarking was perhaps one of the most notable changes to business in the 1970s, one that Malcolm Baldrige valued. This practice of benchmarking began when Xerox's then–corporate president David Kearns gathered key information about competitors to compare marketing and production processes. From this information, he developed benchmarks, or production standards, to improve the quality and manufacturing of copy machines. Xerox's renewed success in the copier market after the use of benchmarking procedures brought the spread of benchmarking to other corporations, including Ford Motor Company and Atlantic Telephone and Telegraph. Although benchmarking brought improved market standing and stock prices for companies that used it, there were significant social consequences, including the firing or forced early retirements of thousands of workers (see Gordon, 1996; Noble, 1994). In spite of these human consequences, benchmarking continued as a valued business practice, and it became a requirement for any recipient of the prestigious Malcolm Baldrige National Quality Award, which honors a company as being "world class."

After Baldrige's death in 1987, the Baldrige model for school reform was created in his honor. Based on Baldrige's business principles, the approach emphasizes decision making based on data accumulated by a school system. This data may include such items as test scores, grades, participation rates in after-school activities, and teachers' salaries. The Baldrige reform model is intended to help educators focus on continuous improvement in student performance (see www.baldridge.org/

Education_Criteria.htm), and it includes seven key criteria: (1) leadership, (2) strategic planning, (3) student and stakeholder focus, (4) information and analysis, (5) faculty and staff focus, (6) process management, and (7) performance results. These key criteria are designed to help educators efficiently plan and implement improvements, align resources, and increase productivity and effectiveness in schools. In and of themselves, these criteria are not necessarily negative things; yet when they are laden with business jargon and situated in a neoliberal milieu, these strategies become dangerous as they potentially divert attention away from public, social concerns toward privatized aims (Giroux, 2003). This became apparent to Mr. Charleson as the Baldridge reform model played out in his school.

Beginning in 1999, an education category was introduced to the competitive Malcolm Baldrige National Quality Award, allowing for-profit and nonprofit public schools and universities to vie for the honor. Three schools became the first education recipients in 2001: (1) the Chugach School District in Anchorage, Alaska; (2) the Pearl River School District in Pearl River, New York; and (3) the University of Wisconsin–Stout in Menomie, Wisconsin. Secretary of Education Rod Paige noted that these education organizations

> made quality, accountability and results hallmarks of their operations, and have set the bar of excellence high for others. I applaud them for their leadership, vision, and most important, commitment to making sure their students receive a high quality education. (U.S. Department of Education, 2001)

Paige's praise reflects what is now an implicit tenet for many in the field of education: Schools are in the business of pleasing consumers, and as such, they must take lessons from the business world in order to run efficient and highly productive organizations. Although a business model may seem to be a good approach to improving U.S. public schools for some, there are important questions about the consequences and effects this logic holds for classrooms, teachers, and students (see, for example, Kohn & Shannon, 2002). Just as benchmarking brought social consequences to the business world, business practices in public schools also bring social consequences to education, teachers, and children. To examine this more closely, we will return to Mr. Charleson's school to consider how business practices have affected education.

Business and Schooling in a Detroit Charter School

As Mr. Charleson explained it to me, the children in his school were workers, and they were referred to as such. The labor they did (tests, assignments, etc.) was compiled as data that was displayed throughout the school on various charts and graphs, much like one would see in industry. In the school's office, colorful charts contained data about the numbers of standards teachers were meeting based on lesson plans they submitted. In classrooms, similar charts displayed student scores and their progress toward standards.

In addition to students being workers in a metaphorical sense, they became actual workers through a Job Corps program. To join the Job Corps program, students needed to prepare a resume and interview for a particular job in the school. After the interview, students began their job, which could involve cleaning the school, delivering lunches, working in the school store, delivering mail, or answering telephones. Teachers and teachers' aides supervised particular jobs, assigning students an average of two hours of work per week. As compensation for their efforts, the children earned school dollars that could be spent at the school store on pencils, candy, and other trinkets. They also could spend their money at special events, such as after-school movies. Children could choose to *not* participate in the Job Corps program, and some children did not participate, but the culture and atmosphere of the school supported this program as the norm.

The adoption of business practices in schools is not a new phenomenon (see Callahan, 1962; Tyack & Cuban, 1995), but that does not make it any less troubling. Fordist models for schools, based on industrial models of production, have been in place since the early part of the 20th century, and although they are considered outdated by many (Cope & Kalantzis, 2000), there is much similarity between industrial models for schools and the models that neoliberals propose (although the socioeconomic and cultural contexts are notably different). Contemporary neoliberal models for education share a fundamental hope with that of old Fordist models; that is, both emphasize efficiency as they expect success in public education to lead to good jobs and good workers that will sustain the U.S. economy.

The emphasis on efficiency has manifested itself in various ways in schools. In reading, basal readers, or basals, which were first published in the 1920s, are one venue to study this emphasis. Across time, basals have been one of the ways in which external forces have controlled the school curriculum, often directing it toward business considerations and needs (Shannon, 1989). Basals take many forms, including basals with supplementary materials, criterion-referenced basals, scripted lessons toward standardized tests, total control programs, and even programs such as Success for All, which is a comprehensive restructuring program for elementary schools that includes systematic reading instruction (see www.successforall.net). Whatever the form, prepackaged reading programs share the goal of making reading instruction more efficient, more uniform, and more legitimate as reading instruction is reified in the materials that are produced (Shannon, 1990), consequently moving the decisions about the teaching of reading away from those who teach reading.

Neoliberalism did not bring deskilling to the teaching of reading; rather, it has continued a trend begun in the earlier part of the 20th century. However, now there are more serious consequences: Today's neoliberal expectations carry a threat to the very existence of public education as a public good. Giroux (2001a) explains:

> Made over in the image of corporate culture, schools are no longer valued as a public good but as a private interest; hence, the appeal of such schools is less in their capacity to educate students according to the demands of critical citizenship than in enabling students to master the requirements of a market-driven economy. Under these circumstances, many students increasingly find themselves in schools that lack any language for relating the self to public life, social responsibility, or the imperatives of democratic life. In this instance, democratic education, with its emphasis on respect for others, critical inquiry, civic courage, and concern for the collective good, is suppressed and replaced by an excessive emphasis on the language of privatization, individualism, self-interest, and brutal competitiveness. (p. 46)

Of course, a contradiction lies in the fact that those who hope to make schools in the image of corporate America cast the necessary requirements for such as "basic skills," rather than emphasizing creativity and intellectual curiosity (Saltman, 2003). This contradiction, in turn, raises important questions about the workers such models intend to produce.

Former Clinton administration Secretary of Labor Robert Reich (2001) predicted that the future U.S. economy will demand workers in the following occupational groups: creative workers (25%); routine production (20%); in-person services (30%); and among the remaining 25%, government employees and farmers, miners, and other "extractors of natural resources" (p. 69). If Reich's estimation holds to be true, and if public schools serve narrow aims required by the job market, the 75% of U.S. citizens who work in areas other than as "creative workers" will likely need basic skills and little more.

For those who believe that public education should serve purposes other than fostering job skills, the notions embedded in a business model for schools are highly problematic. Literacy is important to areas of life other than jobs (see Brandt, 2001; Compton-Lilly, 2003), and more than basic skills are required to educate an informed and participatory citizenry (Shannon, 2002a). It is important to question what modes of social control are at work when the focus of education in general, and literacy education in particular, is limited to basic skills and the "one-right-answer" philosophy that dominates standardized testing and neoliberal visions for schooling.

Absent from business models and neoliberal designs for education are any progressive ideas about what it takes to educate an informed citizenry for participation in a democratic society. Educators such as Dewey (1916) understood free and public education as a social necessity for the renewal of an intellectual, moral, and free democratic society, one that needs to be recreated with each new generation. He noted with concern that

> when we confine the education...to a few years of schooling devoted for the most part to acquiring the use of rudimentary symbols at the expense of training in science, literature, and history...the great majority of workers have no insight into the social aims of their pursuits and no direct personal interest in them. The results actually achieved are not the ends of *their* actions, but only of their employers. They do what they do, not freely and intelligently, but for the sake of the wage earned. It is this fact which makes the action illiberal, and which will make any education

designed simply to give skill in such undertakings illiberal and immoral. (pp. 259–260)

As such, it is important to consider what is missing when schools adopt business models. Gone is any notion of what philosopher Immanuel Kant proposed for education, that is, that children should be educated in accordance with the future, not the present (Kant, 1960). This goal necessarily entails subverting the present to bring about a new and better future condition for the human race, rather than reproducing the present with its social inequities and injustices. Such an education involves critically understanding the present as it relates to the past in order to project a new and better future (Horkheimer, 1974).

In the midst of the Baldrige model for schools and the Job Corps program, Mr. Charleson was responsible for teaching his students a unit on economics. Rather than approach it as a sanitized study of supply, demand, and resources, Mr. Charleson decided to engage students in a study of child labor and child slavery throughout the world. Together, he and his students began to look at the toys and materials in their homes and classroom to see where the products were made and who earned the profits. Mr. Charleson explained that he hoped to foster more than a passive consumerism among his students, teaching them that economics is about more than numbers. Instead, he wanted them to understand that people are behind the numbers and statistics reported in profit and loss statements. He hoped his students would find some parallels between children in other countries and the expectations that they should work to sustain their school. His hopes were realized to some degree when several students understood the concepts well enough that they stopped participating in the Job Corps program. As Mr. Charleson put it, "They knew that being a kid and being a worker wasn't a good thing, or at least shouldn't be synonymous."

Although there are many consequences that can be considered in relation to the corporatization of this Detroit area charter school, there are two related consequences to discuss as we turn finally toward understanding the critical policy study Mr. Charleson employed to make sense of and critique the conditions under which he taught: (1) how the language of the market became the norm in this particular school, leaving little room for critique; and (2) how public space became privatized in this school.

What Are the Consequences of Policy?

As the Baldrige model and the Job Corps program permeated the daily routines of Mr. Charleson's school, there was simultaneously a silent endorsement of consumerism and capitalism as the status quo. Mr. Charleson observed that many of the teachers and students participated unwittingly in these programs because they did not have a language to critique them. In part, this lack could be attributed to the fact that much time was consumed by their labor and on the goal of understanding and implementing the new programs endorsed by the school, giving teachers and students little time to reflect on the ways in which their lives were being shaped by a particular program. In addition, because neoliberal policy is framed in larger social relations, this process in schools presents itself as natural, inevitable, and beneficial, without providing the conditions to systematically question its value to democratic life (see Gee, Hull, & Lankshear, 1997). Apple (2000) refers to this phenomenon as the "intensification" of teachers' work. He explains that the eroding conditions for teaching range in effect from teachers having no time to use the bathroom to them having no time to keep up with their profession. He named consequences of this intensification, among them "cutting corners" so that only the most immediate tasks at hand are completed, which results in overreliance on experts and little time for critical examination of curriculum, textbooks, and more. Apple suggests that this intensification compounds forces already in place to deskill teachers.

For teachers to create the circumstances for their work, they must be in a position to live. Such living involves having time for more than labor and for more than satisfying the basic needs required to make it through a day. However, teachers often feel trapped in the mechanism of their daily work lives. In reference to such possibilities, philosopher Herbert Marcuse (2001) observed that

> individuals must go on spending physical and mental energy in the struggle for existence, status, advantage; they must suffer, service, and enjoy the apparatus which imposes on them this necessity. (p. 65)

Dewey (1916) believed that people need to develop into autonomous and creative individuals who have an understanding of history, social relationships, and productive forces. In this way, individuals' "practical consciousness" (one of the ways Marx [1932/1998] characterized language) is understood as a social product that comes from interactions with others, from shared meanings and understandings of the forces that work to create particular conditions of existence. Such creative and autonomous individuals channel their creativity toward understanding how these meanings are shaped and constructed, not solely toward production and the economy (as Reich would have creativity directed). This creativity is facilitated by having time to reflect and study outside of the time required to earn a living. Marx referred to this as a "realm of freedom" (as cited in McClellan, 2000, p. 535). In this case, freedom is not just leisure time for hobbies and relaxation (freedom from particular responsibilities), but the realm of freedom is also time for unoccupied, quiet time during which individuals can engage their freedom to understand their conditions in new ways, to imagine different and new possibilities for the future. Without this realm, without questioning the language and ideology that policies and programs in our schools embody, we become immune to their meanings and to the political connotations of the language. As a result, we become separated from decisions about our work and susceptible to tendencies that may oppose what we wish schools and education in a participatory, democratic society to be.

The general absence of a language of critique in Mr. Charleson's school allowed the language of the market to become a relatively unquestioned norm. Parents were customers, teachers were supervisors, and children were human capital. The connotations of this language led to the subtle infringement of corporatization into a public space. Where advertising in schools and corporate sponsorship of programs can be an overt and easily recognized movement of business into public education, the language and logic of capitalism and the market often is more elusive with its promises of success (a process replete with winners and losers).

In addition to the language of the market creeping into the school relatively unnoticed, the meaning of the word *work* was grossly subverted. Work involves creating the world beyond our natural surroundings. Philosopher Hannah Arendt (1958) describes three particular forms of human activity: (1) labor, which is what we must engage in to survive; (2) work, or that which is created with our hands and makes up the artificial world; and (3) activity, which involves initiative and the social world (see Table 5 for a summary and brief explanation of Arendt's categories). If we share Arendt's definition of work, children can be characterized as working all the time. Children produce an artificial world as they create ideas, art, music, and more. It is capitalism that subverts the meaning of work to wages, to that which we earn in order to live. At the same time, the ideals and forms of capitalism also are created as part of our artificial world, and we should remember that capitalism can (and has been) changed.

It is important to question the meanings and subversion of language that occur in the authoring and implementation of policies, particularly as we consider the worth of neoliberalism and market-based logic as a model for the U.S. public education system. Will the competition and the implicit acceptance of an unequal playing field that accompanies capitalistic models serve the children in U.S. public schools well? As Kohn (2002) has noted,

> Even the most enlightened businesses, however, are still quite different from what schools are about—or ought to be about. Managers may commit themselves to continuous improvement and try to make their employees' jobs more fulfilling, but the bottom line is that they are still focused on—well, on the bottom line. The emphasis is on results, on turning out a product, on quantifying improvement on a fixed series of measures such as sales volume or return on investment. The extent to which this mentality has taken hold in discussions about education is the extent to which our schools are in trouble. (p. 63)

There has not been any evidence that adopting business models and the corresponding neoliberal ideology (which typically becomes manifest in standards and high-stakes testing as well as the choice movement) in public schools will improve the education and conditions of U.S. children. In other words, although test scores may increase where business models are in place, there is no evidence that learning or education is improved. To the contrary, there is evidence that drop-out rates increase (Orfield & Wald, 2000), that teachers become deskilled technicians (Apple, 2000; Giroux, 2003), and that curricular integrity is compromised while cultural insensitivity is magnified (see Ross & Mathison, 2002). The result is an irrational policy that manipulates the market in the best interests of the wealthy:

TABLE 5	
Arendt's (1958) Categories of Human Activities	
Definition of *Work*	**Explanation**
Labor	• Labor is necessary for life and for society's survival.
	• Labor involves consumption and leaves nothing behind: "the result of its effort is almost as quickly consumed as the effort is spent." (p. 87)
	• People can live without laboring; they can force others to labor for them.
Work	• Work is that which we create with our hands—the human artifice.
	• People might live without working and contributing a useful object to the world.
Activity	• Activity is to begin or to put something in motion.
	• Activity involves speech and requires other people.
	• The space of action and speaking is the public realm, which is kept through power.

The gap between what Americans believe and what they are willing to do also generates policies that are irrational, in the sense that they are inconsistent with or not based on available evidence.... How to explain irrational policymaking? Public officials have at least partly accepted the claim that pursuing the collective goals of the American dream would endanger the individual achievement of children in the majority or privileged sectors. Or they have been persuaded that some panacea exists that would promote the collective good while retaining the privileges of the well-off. (Hochschild, 2001, pp. 36–37)

We must carefully examine the inconsistencies, subversions, and contradictions that these models for public education afford. Mr. Charleson's policy study unpacked this language, and enabled him to critique the neoliberal ideology and business model that permeated his school.

Policy Lessons: Implications for Teachers

From Mr. Charleson's teaching and interactions with the neoliberal policy in his school, we learn that teachers can and do engage critical policy study in interesting ways.

To Mr. Charleson, two aspects of policy study were key:

1. Make time for policy study. As an educator, Mr. Charleson made time for his own "realm of freedom," time when he read books by Henry Giroux, Paulo Freire, Donaldo Macedo, Noam Chomsky, Stanley Aronowitz, Jonathan Kozol, Patrick Shannon, bell hooks, Karl Marx, and others to help him make sense of the conditions and circumstances he was facing. His study also involved writing. Mr. Charleson wrote extensively about his experience in his journal, trying to combine the insights from these scholars with his practical work and theoretical outlook. This study of social issues and ideology, of education and philosophy, coupled with an acute awareness of his own experiences, combined in a way that gave him unique insight into the policies and practices in his school:

> A critical perspective on the policy and school level changes came partly from the theoretical research, but a lot of it came from reflecting on personal experience and practice. I tried to be cognizant of, if not empathetic with, the ways in which certain exercises and classroom management positioned kids and what type of positions would be available to them, and what I would do to make these processes as visible as possible with the students. This came from the personal side: I tried to remember what it felt like to be positioned, especially in a way that was so pervasive and invisible, such as the school plan they were trying to implement. I didn't care for those things when I was a student, and I knew most other students didn't appreciate it either. (personal communication, April 9, 2003)

The goal of this critical study was to bring about social change and an alternative conception of who this teacher and his students were and how they were being produced in this particular context. Critical policy study must pay particular attention, as Mr. Charleson did, to language and its subtleties as the critical policy study works toward a new and different understanding of social conditions, economics, politics, and education. For example, Mr. Charleson took a phenomenon—the market, which usually does not mention human and social components—and revealed the human element of it in his study of child labor. This study, in turn, shed light on the complexities and contradictions of an education system that employs children as workers through the Job Corps program. Mr. Charleson's policy study changed the way he taught, and it changed the way he thought about his teaching and the possible roles of schools under neoliberalism.

2. Connect your policy study with other educators. Policy study may seem to be daunting work, but teachers can begin their policy study in conjunction with other educators. One possibility could be to form extended professional communities through organizations such as the International Reading Association and the National Council of Teachers of English. Some teachers form study groups around books or other professional development activities, and some teachers consider policy. Sometimes schools allow teachers time during their day to engage in these activities (see www.ncrel.org/sdrs/areas/issues/methods/technlgy/te10lk44.htm). At other times, teachers engage in after-school and web-based study groups with other teachers (see www.teachers.net as one of many examples) or e-mail listservs (for example, RTEACHER listserv sponsored by the International Reading Association).

One way Mr. Charleson worked to connect his policy study with other educators was through writing. As his policy study progressed, Mr. Charleson was able to publish his experiences in professional education journals. This act provided him with a way to connect his personal struggles and concerns with others' concerns, to share his policy study in public venues. Such actions are important to bringing social change (see Mills, 1959), as educators share the issues, languages, and contexts of their teaching.

The use of space and time for policy study, as well as the professional connections study groups afford, opens possibilities for a new "realm of freedom" where teachers can engage in policy study that allows them to examine with others how their worlds are constructed, named, and enacted through particular education programs and approaches. Policies never simply and directly flow from the outside of schools to the inside. Instead, policies are negotiated and mediated in light of the values that teachers and others within the school and their related extended and multifaceted professional communities hold (see Coburn, 2001). Because of this, it is never enough to simply accept policies for what they are. Instead, they must be disrupted by questioning the assumptions, definitions, and visions for society that are embedded in them. That is, teachers need to ask, What works for whom? How does it work? What needs to be done to keep children and democracy central to the learning process? In part, this requires a political agency that links theory and practice, one that must be engaged in to "redefine public schooling as a public good and teachers as critical intellectuals whose pedagogical role, in part, is to link learning to social change, but also to join with community and other activists to change social policy" (Giroux, 2003, p. 98).

Detroit is known around the world for its productive automobile industry—Chrysler, Ford, and General Motors. Perhaps for this reason, the language of business is able to creep into schooling in this community without people really wondering much about it. Children do their work, they produce outputs, and they consume. Parents, at least those who have the requisite resources to make informed choices, select schools as customers choose cars: What are the options? Is it affordable? Is it efficient? Do I like the image it portrays of me? Teachers supervise and work to cut costs and excesses. They are rewarded for the value they add to students, as evidenced primarily in test score gains.

Dewey's point that production should be about "free human beings associated with one another on terms of equality" (as cited in Chomsky, 2000, p. 38), rather than merely the production of material goods, certainly seems to be lost in these neoliberal times. To educate free human beings, who can write the world in ways they create, the language of this "new capitalism" will need to be disrupted (see Gee, Hull, & Lankshear, 1997), and our practical consciousness and understandings about its roots and effects will need to be changed. Chomsky (1979) once noted that questions of language also are questions of power. To many, the language of the market has become common sense, and as such, it exerts a powerful influence on U.S. society. Competition is deemed the best means to improve society, and efficiency is prized over all else, sacrificing social goods and services along the way. Are these the same principles that we want to transfer to public education and the children these schools serve? Or should we work instead to create and protect this space from these values that separate and divide us?

CHAPTER 5

On the Way to Somewhere Else: Moving Through Literacy Lessons in a Rural Elementary School

---

CRITICAL POLICY STUDY QUESTIONS ADDRESSED

Who benefits from the policy?

Who is left out?

armen Reed is a Title I teacher (see chapter 2 for background on Title I of the ESEA) in a rural Pennsylvania school. Her school district comprises several rural townships and a small borough, and it serves children from primarily working class families who are employed by a few local manufacturing plants. The community's close proximity to a major highway provides a small influx of "tourists" as people stop in the community on their way to somewhere else, and its proximity to a larger community helps to provide some service jobs. As in many rural communities, life in this area seems to revolve around a mixture of family, work, sporting events, and church.

The elementary school where Ms. Reed teaches is a new facility serving approximately 1,000 students in grades K–5. The school district recently consolidated a handful of smaller and geographically isolated elementary schools that were in older buildings throughout the county. The 2,000 students and approximately 250 full- and part-time professional and support staff in the school district meet in one of three school buildings: the elementary school, the middle school, or the high school.

At the beginning of each school year, Ms. Reed administers tests to determine who will be served by the Title I program. The tests she uses depend on the grade level of the student and may include the Murphy-Durrell Reading Readiness Screen, the Development Reading Assessment, or the Blackburn-Cramp Developmental Writing Scale. The school receives Title I money based on the poverty rate in the district, which was approximately 33% during the 2001–2002 school year. However, the Title I program serves those children who score poorly on the tests Ms. Reed administers, children who are referred to as "at risk," which may or may not include those children who are below the poverty line.

During the 2001–2002 school year, Ms. Reed taught 72 children, a case load comparable to each of the other three Title I teachers in her school. The administration in her school district determined that Ms. Reed should "pick up" 12 children from two of the school's first-grade classrooms, which was nearly the entire class (enrollment was down in the school and first-grade classrooms had an average of 18 children per room). Ms. Reed taught eight children in each of the second- and third-grade classrooms, in addition to "unofficially" working with more children based on their needs. Two classroom aides, whom she needed to train, assisted her as she taught by taking small groups of children and following lesson plans Ms. Reed wrote. Because the aides were not certified teachers (most had a high school diploma only), they were not permitted to write lesson plans or to officially make instructional decisions (even though every engagement with students would necessarily involve decision making).

Ms. Reed's concerns about who benefited from and who was being left out of her school district's reading education policy brought her to initiate policy changes, and her efforts offer some insight about what is needed for policy change at the school and district level. Title I programs are carried out in different ways in different schools, however, and Ms. Reed's experiences are in no way intended to be indicative of Title I programs in all other areas. In addition, Title I is not a program nor is it part of a "reading program" per se (as was the case with silent reading, as discussed in chapter 3), and Title I is not an ideological influence (as was the case with neoliberalism in the Detroit public charter school discussed in chapter 4). Instead, Title I is a funding mechanism, resulting in programs that can look quite different from one school to the next, depending on the money and ideas that inform how it is realized in a given school. Therefore, I have provided more detail about Title I in this particular school, followed by a description of Ms. Reed's efforts to change her school's Title I policy.

Title I Teaching: Moving All the Time

Ms. Reed's Title I teaching was loosely based on a combination of Reading Recovery (Clay, 1990) and Guided Reading (Fountas & Pinnell, 1996). New Zealand educator Marie Clay developed Reading Recovery based on her research in the 1960s and 1970s on young children's early reading difficulties. The program, which uses a one-on-one tutoring model, is targeted toward first-grade children with the goal of lowering the number of young children who have difficulty learning to read and write. The half-hour Reading Recovery lesson follows a format that begins with reading familiar stories, reading a story that was read for the first time the previous day, working with letters and words, writing a story, assembling a cut-up story, and reading a new book. The teacher's responsibility is to provide support and strategies to help the child become successful with reading and writing (see Reading Recovery Council of North America, 2003).

Guided Reading programs have been an effort to take the principles and strategies from Reading Recovery and generalize them to a larger group. Although Ms. Reed was not able to work individually with first graders in her Title I role, she was able to use the tenets of Reading Recovery to inform her 35-minute reading lessons with a small group of six students. Each small-group session involved rereading a familiar story, reading a story that was first read the day before as the teacher collected running record data, and reading a new story. As the children read aloud, Ms. Reed attempted to offer "teaching points," strategies and suggestions to improve the children's ability to read independently. Ms. Reed acknowledged that what her school was calling Guided Reading was not true to the Fountas and Pinnell (1996) explanation. She described this inconsistency as a source of frustration for some teachers who felt that the decisions about their teaching came from the administration's perspectives, rather than the program authors' advice or the teachers' experiences.

As she shared with me her experiences with the Title I program, Ms. Reed described a press to "move" students, teachers, and even herself through the school curriculum and day. Perhaps one of the most explicit goals of the Reading Recovery–Guided Reading model as it was implemented in this rural school involved moving students to the next book and, ultimately, the next reading level. Ms. Reed explained,

> In first grade, we do the Reading Recovery model. We do three books a day in 30 minutes. It's like "whew," so you get to each point and you move and you move on.... It's really hard because you just have to keep them moving the whole time.... All I do is Guided Reading all day. And it helps some of my kids for sure, but for some of my kids I can see it's not working, but yet I can't use other means or other strategies to help them. That's pretty frustrating. (personal communication, September 27, 2002)

While Ms. Reed clearly wanted to advance children in their ability to read independently, she was distraught by the demands the administration placed on her, particularly the three-book-a-day model. She felt this was too much material to cover in 35 minutes with a small group of children, and she wanted to be able to respond to the children's needs in instructive ways. Ms. Reed hoped that she could spend more time teaching the children reading strategies rather than forcing them through three books a day at a quick pace.

In addition to her concern about the fast pace through three books, Ms. Reed felt it was unfortunate that there was never time for writing. Ms. Reed agreed with researchers, such as Albers (2003), Calkins (1994), and others, who have noted the interrelation among reading, writing and other sign systems, and oral language. She found writing to be an important way to teach graphophonic relations, and she knew from prior teaching experiences that it was powerful for children to have the opportunity to read their own writing (see Fullerton & DeFord, 2001, for an explanation of the importance of writing in Reading Recovery lessons). Much like Monaghan and Saul (1987), she questioned the cultural separation of reading and writing that schooling forced on her and her students.

To address her concerns, Ms. Reed set up a meeting with her administration to explain her hopes for change. Much to her disappointment, the administration decided to continue the three-book-a-day schedule. Ms. Reed was told that writing could be done if there was time at the end of the 35-minute lesson, or she could write with children on Fridays when whole-group writing activities were scheduled. After the administration responded to her request, Ms. Reed realized that many of the other teachers were not happy with this decision either. They understood that this was not how reading and writing should be handled, and many of the Title I teachers began to engage children in writing when they knew they would not be observed by the administration. Because of their fear of being caught, however, writing was never taught on a regular basis or in a systematic manner. This raises questions concerning how power was used in this school to control teachers in particular ways.

Moving Teachers

The Title I program in Ms. Reed's school involved a top-down authority that situated power explicitly with the administration. This is not to say that Ms. Reed lacked power or was unable to resist the administration's recommendations; however, as power circulated throughout the school, the recommendations for the program began primarily with the administration, and the consequences for not following their directives were significant. As Ms. Reed explained,

> We get in trouble with the school district if we're not doing exactly what our reading plan says. They say you're going to be put on probation...and then that means that I have to hand in my lesson plan every Friday for the week. So I take that risk. (personal communication, September 27, 2002)

The reading specialists in the school also were responsible for passing on the administrations' directives to the classroom teachers. Ms. Reed was not always comfortable in this role, particularly given teachers' responses to her. She said,

> It's more like the reading staff is dictating the policy down to the classroom teachers...this year there's a lot of resistance from the third-grade teachers because Guided Reading is something new and they're just thrown in. They have one workshop, and then they have another review workshop. They've never done a running record.... They're just used to more traditional grouping, so they don't know how to plan for it...and there is a lot of resentment against certain teachers because they feel that [those teachers] are controlling the whole reading policy. (personal communication, September 27, 2002)

Trying to change these feelings of resentment was hard for Ms. Reed:

> It's hard with the coordination and it's hard to deal with personalities, different personalities, so I tried to be easy, laid back, it's more like "What do you want? I'm here to help out.... This is not my classroom." (personal communication, September 27, 2002)

The classroom teachers' view that they should have been making the decisions about how support was offered to them by the reading specialists is consistent with classroom teachers' expectations in schools throughout the United States (see Quatroche, Bean, & Hamilton, 2001). Research has supported the notion that reading specialists should be collaborative consultants (Henwood, 1999/2000; Jaegar, 1996; Vacca & Padak, 1990); yet the context, structures, and climate of a school can do much to facilitate or discourage this role, resulting in contradictions between administrative expectations and classrooms teachers. As a result, reading specialists such as Ms. Reed hold complex positions that require much negotiation.

In both subtle and overt ways, Ms. Reed experienced a movement of reading teachers away from decisions about their teaching. The consequences of this have manifested in the teachers' general dissatisfaction with their work. Ms. Reed explained,

> The reading department has a huge turnover constantly. I know last year was my first year. More than half of us were new.... I think a lot is because I think people feel, at least with the reading staff, people feel really stifled.... It's very rigorous. Like for me, you can't be creative. It's very rote. (personal communication, September 27, 2002)

Ms. Reed's concerns, which can be characterized as the reification and deskilling of teachers' work, are shared by others across the United States. Duffy (as cited in Powell, 1999) addressed this issue in part during his 1990 presidential address to the National Reading Conference:

> The problem is in the perception—on the part of teachers and those of us trying to help teachers—that instructional power lies not with the minds of teachers but, rather, with programs, procedures, or theories that we create for teachers to follow...we are participating in a system which encourages teachers to compliantly follow rather than to take charge...when we take control away from [teachers] by directing them to follow materials

or codified approaches or tested procedures, we make them into technicians who follow directions. In doing so, we rob them of their professional dignity. (1999, p. 41)

When reading instruction is characterized as a set of procedures, methods, or materials, the human and social elements of reading instruction become minimized or nullified. Such reification works to move teachers away from decisions about their teaching (see Shannon, 1990). The emphasis on technical control in reading teachers' work (in Ms. Reeds case, there is an emphasis on covering three books a day) diminishes the teacher's ability to create lessons for students. At the same time, Shannon (1990) points out that this "deskilling," a focus on the technical rather than the creative, is accompanied instead by a focus on managerial roles. A significant consequence of this work is for teachers to find

> little incentive to improve their knowledge of instruction, of their students, and of educational goals as they at first acquiesce and then project the logic of technical control and reskilling. In this way, many teachers contribute unconsciously to their plight by accepting, and in fact perpetuating, the necessary subjectivity to maintain deskilling in the scientific management of reading instruction.... It is a bad transaction for teachers and an even worse one for students. (p. 154)

In addition to feeling unable to make independent and creative decisions about her teaching, Ms. Reed felt isolated from other teachers who shared her hope to help children read better. In particular, she longed for a professional network of Title I teachers so she could understand the circumstances of their work in relation to hers: "I haven't met any Title I teachers. We don't, unfortunately, have a Title I reading teacher conference, or meet as a group, or [have] any extra [meetings] with [the intermediate unit] or something like that" (personal communication, September 27, 2002). Ms. Reed wanted to be able to learn and try out new ideas based on what others would share, but there was neither time nor space for this to occur.

Moving Self

Ms. Reed's average school day was quite hectic, to say the least. Like many support teachers, the time and space for her work was quite inadequate. She met some children before school began in the morning, children who arrived at school early for the breakfast program. Like many other reading specialists, she felt a responsibility to help all children in the school learn to read better, not just those who were officially assigned to her (see Bean, Cassidy, Grumet, Shelton, & Wallis, 2002).

During the 2001–2002 school year, Ms. Reed's day formally began when she met from 8:50 a.m to 9:25 a.m. with a first-grade class. After this session, she taught from 9:25 a.m. to 10:00 a.m. in a second-grade class, from 10:05 a.m. to 10:40 a.m. in another second-grade class, from 11:00 a.m. to 11:35 a.m. in a third-grade class, and from 11:40 a.m. to 12:15 p.m. in another third-grade class. After a 40-minute lunch, which she often spent gathering materials and supplies for the afternoon, she went to a different first-grade classroom for 35 minutes. She ended the day with a short amount of planning time, which she usually spent giving extra instruction to individual children who needed it most.

Because she was unable to have her own classroom, and because she did not want to lose time by having children travel through the large school building to meet her in her small office, Ms. Reed moved between classrooms carrying a bucket heavy with white boards, markers, and books. She loaded up what she could when she began each day and then changed books for different grades when she had a chance. She admitted that her lessons often ran over the designated 35 minutes, making the pace more hectic as she rushed to meet the next group of students.

Geographer David Harvey (2000) has raised important questions about how space is allocated to serve particular purposes. The allocation of Ms. Reed's work to a small office, to the back of other teachers' classrooms, and to a bucket full of materials sent messages about the meaning of her work. The "unevenness" of her space in the school building in relation to others suggested that her work was peripheral to the regular operations of the school: She was always an intruder in someone else's space, and she was well aware of this. Spatial strategies functioned as an ideological apparatus to control the meanings and functions of Ms. Reed's teaching. In other words, there are spatial barriers between teachers, and between children and teachers, and these barriers work to limit communication among and across these groups in ways that could otherwise bring strategic change to the conditions and structures of public schools.

Perhaps the concerns about space, between "pull-out programs" and "inclusion," would not be quite as alarming if Ms. Reed's time had been less fragmented. Ms. Reed's schedule was determined for her by the school administration, and the use of her time was likewise predetermined. In spite of her experience and advanced education level (she has a master's degree and reading specialist certification), she was not permitted to organize her time and her teaching. As a result, she was always hurrying in and out of other teachers' classrooms, feeling largely unsuccessful in completing the tasks expected of her. Further, there was little to no time for her to forge relationships with the teachers and children in the rooms she visited, or to offer instruction she believed the children needed (e.g., in writing). The conflation of limited space and time leads us to question how human relationships can be nurtured in a field that is very dependent on interrelationships between people. In the end, it seems that neither the teachers nor the reading specialists in Ms. Reed's school district benefited under these conditions. The reading specialists were not part of the decision-making process regarding the instruction their students received, and they were isolated from other teachers in their work. At the same time, they carried out their instruction in short time slots with small groups of children, fearful that they might be caught for not following a lesson plan. This raised questions for Ms. Reed about the possibilities for children to benefit under these instructional conditions.

Questioning Who Benefits: Literacy Learning and Accumulation

Near the beginning of the school year, Ms. Reed held open house sessions to explain the Title I program to parents. However, she often was disappointed with the attendance during these events. She realized that the low attendance was due in part to the difficulties parents had with their work schedules. She explained,

> Next Thursday we have an open house where we talk about what Title I is. We go over the sessions. But, unfortunately, because we have the low kids and we also have the kids with the social problems, too, they might have the parents who might not be involved. The parents might not be able to because [our community] is a blue-collar factory community,

and they might be doing factory jobs at night or something. So, that's a problem. (personal communication, September 27, 2002)

Most of the children Ms. Reed taught were from lower socioeconomic groups, and in addition to Title I services, they typically received speech therapy, occupational therapy, and counseling.

In Ms. Reed's community, there were families for whom schooling had failed for generations to fulfill the promise of a better life and better money, which is a common myth in U.S. culture (Tyack & Cuban, 1995). The literacy instruction Ms. Reed offered seemed to her to be insufficient to change her students' literacy opportunities—their relationships "to social and economic structures that condition chances for learning and development" (Brandt, 2001, p. 7). The social and economic conditions of the children Ms. Reed taught often (but not always) influenced their opportunity to learn and develop as literate citizens. Ms. Reed also felt the literacy instruction she offered would do little to change the literacy development—the "accumulating project of literacy learning across a lifetime, the interrelated effects and potentials of learning over time" (Brandt, 2001, p. 7)—of the children she taught. Over time, literacy learning builds on prior learning, and it crosses generations as one generation's literacy can benefit that of the next generation.

In the end, Ms. Reed felt there was no real literacy learning for her students in the sense that Brandt describes; in other words, there were no "specific occasions" for her students to "take on new understandings or capacities" (p. 6). Instead, they progressed robotically through the motions of reading aloud three books without engaging the meanings, nuances, or contexts of them. Her students had limited opportunity to create and read their own texts, to be given strategic instruction to improve their literacy skills, or to engage in multiple forms of texts and multiliteracies (see Cope & Kalantzis, 2000).

Ms. Reed's fear that these children and these generations of families would not benefit from the Title I instruction offered in her school—that they would not accumulate literacy in the ways their peers and their peer's families did—led her to seek out policy changes. She was acutely aware of the ways in which literacy instruction, "schooled literacy," involved moral choices (Powell, 1999), and she was morally committed to bringing change for the children she taught. She believed literacy learning was central to the possibilities for social change in her students' lives. With this in mind, she approached her administration and expressed her concerns about the limitations of the three-book-a-day method, the lack of writing instruction, and the need for human engagement in her teaching. She did not expect she would experience change in her teaching space or the hectic pace, and she decided to begin with questions that were of most concern to her, questions she thought could be reasonably addressed.

Policy Lessons: Implications for Teachers

Although Ms. Reed was not as successful as she had hoped to be in changing the policy for the Title I program in her school, she felt she learned some important lessons about policy implementation and change that would increase her chances of changing policy in the future. She felt she made an important beginning in communicating with her administration about policy change, and she expected that some changes in her own approach would help her to be more successful in the future. In particular, she had the following advice for other teachers:

1. Be knowledgeable about research and policy. After her meeting with the administration, Ms. Reed understood that she needed evidence to support her claims that instructional time with the children should be handled differently. She needed to help her administration to understand theories and methods of literacy instruction so they could make informed decisions about reading instruction in the school. It was not enough for her to say, "This is what I think." Instead, she needed to say, "Here's what I know based on this research, and in light of this research, here's what we need to do." Further support for Ms. Reed's insight about the importance of research and policy understandings in her work comes from Vogt and Shearer (2003), who encourage reading specialists to be "independent, critical examiners of events, issues, and policies in literacy education" (p. 18).

2. Join up with others. Ms. Reed also believed that she would have had more influence if she had organized with other teachers before approaching her administration. This organization would have shown the administration that her concerns were not hers alone, but that others shared her hopes for change. Dewey (1916) explained that the voluntary associations to which we belong can do much to bring about societal changes, and it seems this tenet holds true in education settings and policy situations as well. Likewise, this association can cross schools and settings, particularly where Title I teaching is concerned. Quatroche, Bean, and Hamilton (2001) recommend that reading specialists establish a network that allows them to work collaboratively as they try to understand and carry out the complexities of their roles in schools. Ms. Reed's hope for a network of Title I reading teachers seems as though it would fill a much-needed void, one that could offer professional development, instructional assistance, and policy advocacy.

3. Create spaces of hope. In addition to a stronger union with the other reading teachers in the school, Ms. Reed felt the collaboration between the classroom teachers and the reading specialists could be stronger and more effective. One of the ways this partnership could happen is by setting aside collaborative time for these two groups of educators (Quatroche, Bean, & Hamilton, 2001), allowing time for them to communicate with each other about instructional concerns and issues. Different uses of space and time are needed in Ms. Reed's situation, and there are ways these spaces, or "literacy communities," can be made without too much change to the regular schedule in the school (see Vogt & Shearer, 2003). In addition, technology can help to create these spaces of hope through e-mail listservs, chat rooms, and so on to provide avenues for teachers to communicate with and learn from one another.

Ms. Reed's knowledge of reading instruction, her concern for the children she was responsible for teaching, and her moral commitment to literacy learning led her to seek policy change in her school. Although her first attempts at policy change did not garner the results for which she had hoped, she learned from the experience and planned to return to the administration with new and different ideas for change in her school. When she returned, she planned to have evidence from research to back her claims, support from other teachers in the school, and ideas for continued collaboration between classroom teachers and reading specialists as they worked together to generate new and better instruction for the children and conditions for their work.

CHAPTER 6

Policy Study and Policy Action: What Might Teachers Do?

The critical policy study in this book considers current education policies in relation to the historical context of the original ESEA, and it situates these policies in relation to current trends (such as neoliberalism) and programs (such as Guided Reading). This discussion reflects an assumption that teachers control and work with policy daily, and their choices of "what to do" must be knowledgeable in relation to their contexts and situations. For this reason, this book emphasizes critical policy study as a starting place for responding to and working with policies.

The federal government will continue to play a role in U.S. public education, including literacy policies, and this role will continue to influence state, district, and classroom policies. Therefore, it is perhaps more important than ever for educators to critically understand and engage in policy, particularly if we hope for education policy that guarantees that people's Fourteenth Amendment rights are protected. Poverty, racism, inadequate school buildings and resources, insufficient space and time for teachers' intellectual work, and other factors continue to challenge the possibilities for providing equal educational opportunities for children and appropriate work conditions for teachers in U.S. public schools, and teachers are better positioned than any other group to make these needs known. Much work needs to be done toward this end, and much effort needs to be expended toward including teachers in policymaking processes at state and federal levels. If we are committed to the purposes and aims of public education in a democratic society, however, we cannot sit idly by, allowing mobilization of biases to direct policy discussions in some areas while ignoring others. Instead, we need to become involved in policy study and policymaking in order to effect changes that will benefit the children in U.S. public schools. For this reason, we will consider three general possibilities for policy involvement: (1) engaging in critical policy study, (2) educating the public, and (3) imagining new possibilities. (See Table 6 for a summary of policy activities.)

TABLE 6	
Summary of Policy Activities Teachers Can Do	
Activity	Description
Engaging in Critical Policy Study	• Functionalist study asks what the measurable effects of a policy are, and it focuses on works within a particular context. As teachers, we can learn from functionalist study, but we must not stop with these questions.
	• Critical policy study considers where a policy has come from; the social, historical, and political aspects of policy; the values and definitions of a policy's author(s); the consequences of policy; and who benefits from and who is left out of a policy (see Edmondson, 2002). This study will help teachers to raise different questions about policy and its consequences.
Educating the Public	• Teachers can be engaged as "public intellectuals" (Giroux, 1988) who help to inform their communities about particular policies and their effects. Participation can take many forms, including writing in local newspapers, speaking in public town and school board meetings, holding workshops for teachers and parents, and inviting local legislators into the classroom.
Imagining New Possibilities	As educators, we can
	• seek wide civic participation through our own civic engagement;
	• respect differences as we seek consensus across values and respect different positions;
	• formulate new identities, choices, and alternatives for literacy education; and
	• open new political spaces where we can discuss, debate, and influence federal policy.

Engaging in Critical Policy Study

As the examples throughout this book demonstrate, teachers can and do engage in critical policy study. This study often begins with a hunch that something is not quite right; in other words, teachers often come to critical policy study, just as Mr. Roberts and Mr. Charleson did, through the filter of their own experiences and recognition of the seeming contradiction between policies and their own beliefs and knowledge about literacy teaching and learning. If we as educators consider the contradictions between policies and our own beliefs about literacy more closely, we can engage in critical policy study and open avenues for policy change. Specifically, we can turn to the critical policy questions that were introduced in chapter 1 as a starting place for our inquiries into policy.

In chapter 2, we discussed the origins of policy, including the social, historical, and political aspects of it. To do so, we considered the influences of the Civil Rights movement on the original ESEA. By situating this policy within a particular time and place, we were able to see the liberal enlightenment ideals that influenced the original legislation, ideals that were never fully realized. In part, they were not realized because of the limitations of social policies that accompanied the time period (including Marcuse's concern about the contradictions inherent in the Great Society in general—the belief that the affluent would change the social conditions that led to and protected their affluence), along with limited and limiting definitions of poverty and narrow understandings of racism (Prendergast, 2003). Yet the ESEA has continued to play a strong role in debates and discussions about the federal government's role in education. Throughout the decades since the original ESEA, the policy has been directed differently depending on *who* the policymakers were and what their values were. Across the same time period, there have been teachers, such as those Heath (1983) describes, who have agreed with the tenets of the policy and attempted to improve their teaching in relation to it, and there have been teachers, such as Dan Roberts, who have believed that their teaching practices were more effective for their students than those outlined in the policy.

As neoliberalism gained influence throughout the 1990s, literacy education became increasingly viewed as a key component of a "success equation" that would lead to a well-educated work force that would secure the United States's position in a globalized economy. Throughout this period, business groups became increasingly influential in U.S. public schools, and teachers, such as Rob Charleson, began to question the underlying assumptions and definitions in the program they were expected to implement. Essentializing race by treating ethnic and cultural groups as monolithic rather than diverse (see Mendez, 2001), along with attempting to homogenize or assimilate Americans into a normalized view of "community," certainly influenced the way in which federal policy was articulated. Many teachers wondered about the consequences of policy for their schools and communities, and the children they taught. Dan Roberts, and teachers like him who hoped to nurture a love of reading, found contradictions between their practices and the practices detailed by scientifically based research. Carmen Reed wondered about the benefits of her teaching practices in relation to economically devastated families in her community who did not seem to be given the opportunity to "accumulate" literacy. All the teachers described in this book wondered who would be left out if current policies, and practices in relation to these policies, continued, and they all, including the teachers in Heath's (1983) research, began some movement toward change.

Teachers should be assured that their own concerns about the differences between their beliefs about literacy education and the current policies for literacy education are important places to begin to study policy and to bring about policy change. Policy change can begin with individuals—Heath's teachers, Dan Roberts, Rob Charleson, and Carmen Reed have shown this; however, change cannot end with individuals. Educators must begin to link their concerns with one another and work together to strategically influence policies at all levels: local, state, and federal.

Societal change is a long and arduous process, and educators must be committed to such an effort for the long term. One possibility for beginning such efforts is for teachers to join together in study groups that focus on policy texts. In some school districts, teachers are allocated time during the school day to engage in such study groups (see http://teachers.net/gazette/AUG00/fisher.html for an account of one school-based teacher study group). The study groups can direct teachers' attention to policy issues and policy change. For example, teachers could read together the Report of the National Reading Panel (NICHD, 2000), considering it in relation to the Reading First program. They could read texts that engage different perspectives of the NRP report (such as Coles, 2003; Cunningham, 2001; Garan, 2002) and make decisions about their own beliefs in relation to the values inherent in the NRP report and the No Child Left Behind Act. In this way, teachers can become more informed about the policy, and they can explain their compliance with it or their resistance to it in informed ways that will allow them to link their efforts with other groups and educators.

In addition, teachers can engage in after-school and web-based study groups with other teachers (see www.commtechlab.msu.edu/ site/letsnet/noframes/bigideas/b9/b9u4.html for an explanation of how to form teacher study groups; see also www.teachers.net for examples of online discussions among teachers). There are many electronic mailing lists (for example, the RTEACHER listserv sponsored by the International Reading Association) that provide opportunities for teachers to communicate with educators throughout the world. These electronic communication tools have the potential to play a significant role in effecting social and educational change, and they also potentially provide a terrific opportunity to inform the general public about education issues and educators' concerns. The public, particularly parents of school-age children, can be influential across all levels of policy, including but not limited to their votes for school board members, local representatives, and state and federal officials. Yet there is much work that needs to be done in order to engage the public in strategic ways.

Educating the Public

Public Agenda—a nonpartisan and nonprofit research organization founded in 1975—released a report in 2003 titled *Where We Are Now: 12 Things You Need to Know About Public Opinion and Public Schools*. Underwritten by Washington Mutual, the report is based on more than a dozen national surveys taken by parents, teachers, students, principals, superintendents, and school boards from 1998 to 2000. Although there is not space in this chapter to adequately investigate questions related to this document (for instance, why a bank would underwrite such a project), it is interesting for our purposes to note that the authors of the report suggest that public opinion should not play a role in policy change, largely because

> people are not following some important debates in education very close-
> ly. They may have a vision of the kind of public schools they want, but

few have struggled with the details of precisely how to get there. Parents are understandably more focused on the needs of their own child than on those of children overall.... It is also worth remembering that some of the most significant developments in American history have not been led by public opinion. Americans now say that the civil rights movement benefited the country, but that was not always the case. (pp. 6–7)

The report points to discrepancies in parents' and educators' understandings and opinions. For example, the discussion of the findings opens with the following statement: "The specific provisions of the No Child Left Behind Act may be controversial among educators, but the public's support for the ideas behind the drive to raise standards is not in doubt" (p. 8). If this statement concerns us, and if it is true that the public does not understand education policy issues in the same way that educators do, then we should be doing something to change these understandings. It seems to me that the previously discussed points about engaging in policy study, working locally, and taking alternative positions should help to direct us. In other words, we need to critically understand policy, help others to understand it, and employ our sociological imaginations to offer alternatives to and new ideas for policy.

As each of the three teachers in this book have demonstrated, we as educators can and should work to educate the public about needs and concerns in our schools and communities. Although there are many ways to do this, the following two areas in particular were evident in these teachers' work: (1) engaging policy change in their classrooms and communities, and (2) writing articles and teaching accounts for other educators and the public.

Engaging Policy Change in Classrooms and Communities

Mr. Roberts's silent protest of the silent reading policy in his school began policy change from the classroom level. His effort educated children, parents, and other teachers and began to spread through the school as others heard about his protest and discussed the silent reading policy with him. Grassroots efforts for policy change can be one effective way to begin policy change processes.

As policy change spreads from classrooms to other arenas throughout school districts, states, and the United States at large, there are various voluntary associations that can be formed to influence policy. For example, citizens groups have come together to educate the public about pressing issues and to subsequently effect changes in their communities. In "Prairie Town," Minnesota, for example, townspeople, educators, and high school students came together to decide how best to live together and survive in light of the neoliberal influences on their community. The ongoing farm crisis and government policies in agriculture and education threatened to erase them and the community's school from the map (see Edmondson, 2003, for more specifics on these policies and conditions).

During the first set of town meetings in Prairie Town, the people participating developed a vision statement to guide their work. The vision statement articulated goals in areas of economic opportunity, recreation and culture, community leadership, infrastructure and services, lifelong learning, and the valuing of diversity. The subtheme of the meetings, as articulated in a narrative written by the project coordinator, included

> connecting our community, first to itself, and then to the world. The designated projects all foster a connection of people to people, people to resources, and our community to the surrounding communities. Having successfully constructed a strong infrastructure of service, support, and accessibility the community is equipped to reach beyond its borders and impact a wider world. (Edmondson, 2003, p. 100)

This visioning process was followed by a series of meetings that brought people from four generations together to help the community move toward their vision. Their vision was not just about nostalgia for the old days but was a look toward a future that would link the community to the world in ways that community members defined. It involved generating shared languages and literacies as people worked to read their current circumstances in public forums that addressed pressing conditions (including employment rates, infrastructure needs, technological concerns, and more). Participation in these planning meetings, in turn, involved employing a variety of literacies as people made decisions together that would eventually bring about changes to their community. Today, teachers in Prairie Town continue to be instrumental in this process as they inform local community members about infrastructure and programmatic needs, and trends among students. Although this process is still ongoing, there have been positive changes, including consensus from a community vote for a new elementary school building, new recreational activities for young people in the town, and a renewed emphasis on local history and art (see Edmondson, 2003, for a more detailed account).

These initial Prairie Town meetings engaged different literacies than those endorsed by neoliberal perspectives, and they required townspeople, along with teachers, to have different understandings of literacy and language to negotiate and inform the public about the relation between the school and the community. At the same time, these meetings did much to inform the local citizenry about education issues, which ultimately influenced their nominations and votes for school board members, as well as their choices for local, state, and federal representatives. In this way, the teachers worked as "public intellectuals" (Giroux, 1988, pp. 72–73) who understood the issues and challenges of education in their community and engaged in educating the public at large about these issues.

Writing for Policy Change

Writing can be another integral way to engage policy study and begin policy change. Mr. Charleson wrote for himself in a journal and wrote for others by publishing articles in professional journals. His personal writing helped him to sort through the various initiatives in and influences on his school, and it allowed him to organize the readings he engaged. As he sifted through information about neoliberalism, business models for schooling, and the economy, he eventually began to write for others as he organized his writing into articles for publication. This linking of his private story to public issues is important in helping others to realize that situations they face are not theirs alone. In other words, these are not individual problems but are social issues instead. The organization of teachers' time by others, the deskilling of teachers, and ineffective literacy instruction concern teachers and communities broadly. Writing in the local newspaper, posting comments on the Internet, or starting a newsletter to unite Title I teachers are a few possible ways for teachers to use writing to address policy concerns.

Imagining New Possibilities

Political ideologies are socially constructed, as are the groups that policies are meant to address (Schneider & Ingram, 1997). We do not have to subscribe to the political ideologies that are dominant in today's society. Instead, we can work outside the existing ideologies to create new spaces and new possibilities. Participating in political processes and policy study does much to increase the political consciousness and awareness of those involved (see Friere, 1972, for one of many examples of raising consciousness through education; see also Clegg, 1989).

Powell (1999) notes that discussions about the type of society we would like to create together are largely absent from discussions about education reform. The development of a democratic vision, one that would help us to think about how we might live together, should be central to our policy study and policy work. Such discussions necessarily involve the engagement of different positions and require the employment of a sociological imagination (Mills, 1959) to offer alternatives to current policies. These discussions should give us hope as we work to change the social conditions and problems that have resulted from economic inequities and policies that have not adequately addressed issues of race and class in the United States. As Shannon (1998) explains,

> the traditional rationales for schooling and reading education are no longer viable, and we must rethink both; that is, unless we are willing to consciously serve cultural and economic injustices. Under these conditions, issues of recognition and redistribution that have been heretofore unthinkable now deserve our attention, careful consideration, and action. We must develop new ways of thinking about poverty, schooling, and ourselves. Moreover, we must build new partnerships for doing that thinking to garner enough power to transform structures, as well as help individuals. (pp. 201–202)

Critical policy study is integral to effecting these changes as we work to develop new understandings and new possibilities for public education in general and literacy education specifically.

Conclusion

As reading teachers, our critical policy study, our work to educate the public about literacy instruction in our classrooms, and our efforts to construct new and different understandings of literacy and ideology in our globalized society are more important than ever. Yet this is not to suggest that we should always agree or that we should expect to arrive at a consensus about each issue. With any truly democratic project, there is always dissent and compromise, and there is always change. However, we can work to change the meanings that are attached to our lives, and we can change the ways in which we come to understand and read the world as we work to write it anew.

Dewey (1916) emphasizes in his philosophical and educational writings that each generation needs to define and redefine democracy. Central to this effort to redefine democracy is an education that offers opportunities for students to examine and understand the link between democracy and education, affording them the opportunity to socially reconstruct democracy and its policies in light of current contexts and situations (see Dewey, 1916; Shannon, 1990). Projects that are democratic, as any critical policy study should be, are difficult work as we learn to consider and respect our differences with others, and to understand how these differences matter. This understanding is not so we can put differences aside but so that we can begin to forge an understanding of our collective social needs. Literacy is central to every aspect of this work as we attempt to critically understand languages, meanings, and texts.

Engagement in critical policy study that considers the historical origins, social contexts, and values of policies, as well as alternative positions, can lead us to historical, economic, cultural, and social understandings of the meanings and needs facing literacy education. Such study is a crucial first step in our work toward recognizing what is valuable about certain policies as we simultaneously strive to bring about policy changes. The findings of our critical policy study should, in turn, allow us to respectfully and publicly raise our support or objection to particular policies or aspects of policies as we help to educate others about the cultural meanings and understandings that are reflected in the policies. Such work should strive to be publicly relevant because we hope to educate parents and others in our communities (geographic and professional) about the meanings we share, those we do not, and why. This, in turn, can open spaces for the discussion of different possibilities that should influence our school boards, state and federal legislators, and the policies and meanings that affect our schools.

APPENDIX

Policy-Related Resources
for Further Study

Suggested Readings on Policy and Policy Study

Business Influences in Schools

Gee, J., Hull, G., & Lankshear, C. (1997). *The new work order: Behind the language of the new capitalism.* Boulder, CO: Westview Press.

Kohn, A., & Shannon, P. (2002). *Education, Inc.: Turning learning into a business* (Rev. ed.). Portsmouth, NH: Heinemann.

Marshall, R., & Tucker, M. (1992). *Thinking for a living: Education and the wealth of nations.* New York: Basic Books.

Molnar, A. (1996). *Giving kids the business: The commercialization of America's schools.* Boulder, CO: Westview Press.

Saltman, K.J. (2001). *Collateral damage: Corporatizing public schools—A threat to democracy.* Lanham, MD: Rowman & Littlefield.

Shannon, P. (2001). *iSHOP, you shop: Raising questions about reading commodities.* Portsmouth, NH: Heinemann.

Critical Policy Study

Edmondson, J. (2000). *America Reads: A critical policy analysis.* Newark, DE: International Reading Association.

Fowler, F.C. (2000). *Policy studies for educational leaders: An introduction.* Upper Saddle River, NJ: Pearson Education.

Marshall, C. (1997). *Feminist critical policy analysis I: A perspective from primary and secondary schooling.* London: Falmer.

Ozga, J. (1999). *Policy research in educational settings: Contested terrain.* Buckingham, UK: Open University Press.

Prunty, J.J. (1985). Signposts for a critical educational policy analysis. *Australian Journal of Education, 29*(2), 133–140.

Critical Theory

Giroux, H.A. (2001). *Theory and resistance in education: Toward a pedagogy for the opposition* (Rev. ed.). Westport, CT: Greenwood.

Jay, M. (1996). *The dialectical imagination: A history of the Frankfurt School and the Institute of Social Research, 1923–1950.* Berkeley: University of California Press.

Marcuse, H. (1964). *One dimensional man: Studies in the ideology of advanced industrial society.* Boston: Beacon.

Parker, L., Deyhle, D., & Villenas, S. (Eds.). (1999). *Race is…race isn't: Critical race theory and qualitative studies in education*. Boulder, CO: Westview Press.

Education and Democracy

Ayers, W., Hunt, J.A., & Quinn, T. (Eds.). (1998). *Teaching for social justice: A democracy and education reader*. New York: New Press.

Dewey, J. (1916). *Democracy and education*. New York: Free Press.

Gutmann, A. (1999). *Democratic education* (Rev. ed.). Princeton, NJ: Princeton University Press.

Mills, C.W. (1959). *The sociological imagination*. London: Oxford University Press.

Sehr, D.T. (1997). *Education for public democracy*. Albany: State University of New York Press.

Shannon, P. (1990). *The struggle to continue: Progressive reading instruction in the United States*. Portsmouth, NH: Heinemann.

Swift, R. (2002). *The no-nonsense guide to democracy*. New York: Verso.

Government Reports on Reading and Public Education

Adams, M.J. (1990). *Beginning to read: Thinking and learning about print*. Cambridge, MA: MIT Press.

Anderson, R.C., Hiebert, E.H., Scott, J.A., & Wilkinson, I.A.G. (1985). *Becoming a nation of readers: The report of the Commission on Reading*. Washington, DC: National Institute of Education.

National Commission on Excellence in Education. (1983). *A nation at risk: The imperative for educational reform*. Washington, DC: U.S. Department of Education.

National Institute of Child Health and Human Development (NICHD). (2000). *Report of the National Reading Panel. Teaching children to read: An evidence-based assessment of the scientific research literature on reading and its implications for reading instruction* (NIH Publication No. 00-4769). Washington, DC: U.S. Government Printing Office.

Snow, C., Burns, S., & Griffin, P. (1998). *Preventing reading difficulties in young children*. Washington, DC: National Academy Press.

Policy and Policymaking

Allington, R.L. (2002). *Big brother and the national reading curriculum: How ideology trumped evidence*. Portsmouth, NH: Heinemann.

Ball, S.J. (1990). *Politics and policy making in education: Explorations in policy sociology.* New York: Routledge.

Coles, G. (2000). *Misreading reading: The bad science that hurts children.* Portsmouth, NH: Heinemann.

Coles, G. (2003). *Reading the naked truth: Literacy, legislation, and lies.* Portsmouth, NH: Heinemann.

Fowler, F.C. (2000). *Policy studies for educational leaders: An introduction.* Upper Saddle River, NJ: Pearson Education.

Garan, E.M. (2002). *Resisting reading mandates: How to triumph with the truth.* Portsmouth, NH: Heinemann.

Heath, S.B. (1983). *Ways with words: Language, life, and work in communities and classrooms.* Cambridge, UK: Cambridge University Press.

Sabatier, P. (Ed.). (1999). *Theories of the policy process.* Boulder, CO: Westview Press.

Schneider, A.L., & Ingram, H. (1997). *Policy design for democracy.* Lawrence: University of Kansas Press.

Smith, F. (2003). *Unspeakable acts, unnatural practices: Flaws and fallacies in "scientific" reading instruction.* Portsmouth, NH: Heinemann.

Taylor, D. (1998). *Beginning to read and the spin doctors of science: The political campaign to change America's mind about how children learn to read.* Urbana, IL: National Council of Teachers of English.

Theodoulou, S., & Cahn, M. (1995). *Public policy: The essential readings.* Englewood Cliffs, NJ: Prentice Hall.

Tyack, D.B., & Cuban, L. (1995). *Tinkering toward utopia: A century of public school reform.* Cambridge, MA: Harvard University Press.

Political Influences on Literacy Education and Education Policy

Apple, M.W. (2000). *Official knowledge: Democratic education in a conservative age.* New York: Routledge.

Chomsky, N. (with Macedo, D., Ed.). (2000). *Chomsky on miseducation.* Boulder, CO: Rowman & Littlefield.

Fraatz, J.M.B. (1987). *The politics of reading.* New York: Teachers College Press.

Macedo, D.P. (1994). *Literacies of power: What Americans are not allowed to know.* Boulder, CO: Westview Press.

Powell, R.L. (1999). *Literacy as a moral imperative: Facing the challenges of a pluralistic society.* Lanham, MD: Rowman & Littlefield.

Shannon, P. (Ed.). (2001). *Becoming political, too: New readings and writings on the politics of literacy education.* Portsmouth, NH: Heinemann.

Spring, J. (2001). *Conflicts of interest: The politics of American education* (4th ed.). New York: McGraw-Hill.

Political Orientations

Overview

Spring, J. (1997). *Political agendas in education: From the Christian Coalition to the Green Party.* Hillsdale, NJ: Erlbaum.

From Conservative Perspective

D'Souza, D. (1991). *Illiberal education: The politics of sex and race on campus.* New York: Free Press.

Dunn, C.W., & Woodard, J.D. (2003). *The conservative tradition in America* (Rev. ed.). Boulder, CO: Rowman & Littlefield.

Kirk, R. (Ed.). (1996). *The portable conservative reader.* New York: Viking.

Kirk, R. (2001). *The conservative mind: From Burke to Eliot* (7th ed.). Washington, DC: Regnery.

From Liberal Perspective

Rawls, J. (1996). *Political liberalism.* New York: Columbia University Press.

Rousseau, J. (1968). *The social contract.* New York: Penguin. (Original work published 1791)

From Neoconservative Perspective

Gerson, M. (1996). *The neoconservative vision: From the cold war to the culture wars.* Lanham, MD: Rowman & Littlefield.

Gerson, M. (1997). *The essential neoconservative reader.* Reading, MA: Addison-Wesley.

Kristol, I. (1995). *Neoconservativism: Selected essays 1949–1995.* New York: Free Press.

From Neoliberal Perspective

Friedman, M. (2002). *Capitalism and freedom: Fortieth anniversary edition.* Chicago: University of Chicago Press.

Marshall, R., & Tucker, M. (1992). *Thinking for a living: Education and the wealth of nations.* New York: Basic Books.

Reich, R.B. (2001). *The future of success.* New York: Knopf.

From Radical Democratic Perspective

Laclau, E., & Mouffe, C. (2001). *Hegemony and socialist strategy: Towards a radical democratic politics* (2nd ed.). New York: Verso.

Shannon, P. (Ed.). (2001). *Becoming political, too: New readings and writings on the politics of literacy education.* Portsmouth, NH: Heinemann.

Trend, D. (Ed.). (1996). *Radical democracy: Identity, citizenship, and the state.* London: Routledge.

Race, Poverty, Gender, and Inequality

Delpit, L.D. (1995). *Other people's children: Cultural conflict in the classroom.* New York: New Press.

Finders, M. (1997). *Just girls: Hidden literacies and life in junior high* (Language and Literacy series). Urbana, IL: National Council of Teachers of English.

Freire, P. (1972). *The pedagogy of the oppressed* (D. Macedo, Trans.). New York: Penguin.

Giroux, H.A. (2003). *The abandoned generation: Democracy beyond the culture of fear.* New York: Palgrave MacMillan.

Gonick, M. (2003). *Between femininities: Ambivalence, identity, and the education of girls.* Albany: State University of New York Press.

Gooding-Williams, R. (1993). *Reading Rodney King: Reading urban uprising.* New York: Routledge.

Kelley, R.D.G., & Lewis, E. (Eds.). *To make our world anew: A history of African Americans.* New York: Oxford University Press.

Kozol, J. (1991). *Savage inequalities: Children in America's schools.* New York: Crown.

Prendergast, C.C. (2003). *Literacy and racial justice: The politics of learning after* Brown v. Board of Education. Carbondale: Southern Illinois University Press.

Shannon, P. (1998). *Reading poverty.* Portsmouth, NH: Heinemann.

Taylor, D. (1996). *Toxic literacies: Exposing the injustice of bureaucratic texts.* Portsmouth, NH: Heinemann.

Winant, H. (2001). *The world is a ghetto: Race and democracy since World War II.* New York: Basic Books.

Professional Organizations and Education Advocacy Groups

International Reading Association
www.reading.org
302-731-1600

> The International Reading Association is a professional association of educators, with over 300,000 members and affiliates in 99 countries. Five primary goals of the Association include professional development, advocacy, partnerships, research, and global literacy development. The association publishes peer-reviewed journals—*The Reading Teacher*, *Journal of Adolescent & Adult Literacy*, *Peremena/Thinking Classroom*, *Lectura y Vida*, and *Reading Research Quarterly*—as well as books, position statements, and a membership newspaper, *Reading Today*. The Association also publishes position statements on issues affecting public policy, and it holds annual government relations workshops, in addition to international, national, and regional conferences.

National Council of Teachers of English
www.ncte.org
877-369-6283

> With 77,000 members in the United States and other countries, NCTE's mission is to promote "the development of literacy, the use of language to construct personal and public worlds and to achieve full participation in society, through the learning and teaching of English and the related arts and sciences of languages" (8/90 Strategic Plan). The Council's publications include journals, such as *Language Arts*, *English Journal*, and *College English*, as well as books, position statements on public policy issues, and a membership newspaper, *The Council Chronicle*. A national conference is held annually, and NCTE also holds regional and affiliate meetings.

National Reading Conference
www.nrconline.org
414-768-8000

> The National Reading Conference is a professional organization for people who are interested in literacy and literacy education. The organization's mission is to support the professional development of emerging and established scholars, and to advocate for research-informed improvements in education. The organization sponsors an annual conference, a yearbook that publishes studies reported at the conference, and *The Journal of Literacy Research*. It also publishes white papers to inform readers about policy issues related to reading research.

Websites and Online Publications

Education Policy Analysis Archives (http://epaa.asu.edu)
> This electronic peer-reviewed journal is edited by Gene V. Glass, Professor in the College of Education at Arizona State University. The journal offers scholarly analyses and discussions of policies and policy issues.

Education Week (www.edweek.org)
> This weekly publication offers current news and updates on national and international issues on education. The website contains links to archives and *Teacher* magazine.

Reading Online (www.readingonline.org)
> *Reading Online* is an entirely online journal of practice and research for K–12 teachers and is published by the International Reading Association. There are peer-reviewed articles, an "electronic classroom," discussions of new literacies (e.g., media literacy), and online communities for teachers to join.

Rethinking Schools (www.rethinkingschools.org)
> This publication was begun in 1986 by a group of teachers who were interested in influencing reform in the U.S. public school system. It is offered quarterly with articles written by teachers, students, and activists. There also are other publications offered by this group, such as *Rethinking Schools: An Agenda for Change* and *Rethinking School Reform: Views From the Classroom.*

Thomas: Legislative Information on the Internet (http://thomas.loc.gov)
> This website contains Library of Congress information, full texts and summaries of House and Senate bills, historical information and documents, and information on how to contact your state representatives. There also is useful information about the law-making process, historical documents, and details on the executive and judicial branches of the U.S. federal government.

U.S. Department of Education (www.ed.gov)
> The U.S. Department of Education's website contains links to legislation, policy, research, grants, and more. It also offers access to archived information from past presidential administrations.

REFERENCES

Albers, P. (2003). Integrating a semiotic view of literacy. In J.C. Richards & M.C. McKenna (Eds.), *Integrating multiple literacies in K–8 classrooms* (pp. 150–171). Mahwah, NJ: Erlbaum.

Allington, R.L. (2002). *Big brother and the national reading curriculum: How ideology trumped evidence.* Portsmouth, NH: Heinemann.

America Reads Challenge Act of 1997, S. 664, 105th Cong. (1997).

Anderson, R.C., Hiebert, E.H., Scott, J.A., & Wilkinson, I.A.G. (1985). *Becoming a nation of readers: The report of the Commission on Reading.* Washington, DC: National Institute of Education.

Apple, M.W. (2000). *Official knowledge: Democratic education in a conservative age.* New York: Routledge.

Arendt, H. (1958). *The human condition.* Chicago: University of Chicago Press.

Arendt, H. (1968). *Men in dark times.* Orlando, FL: Harcourt Brace.

Aronowitz, S. (1988). *Science as power: Discourse and ideology in modern society.* Minneapolis: University of Minnesota Press.

Ball, S.J. (1990). *Politics and policy making in education: Explorations in policy sociology.* New York: Routledge.

Bean, R.M., Cassidy, J., Grumet, J.E., Shelton, D.S., & Wallis, S.R. (2002). What do reading specialists do? Results from a national survey. *The Reading Teacher, 55,* 736–744.

Bell, D. (1995). *Brown v. Board of Education* and the interest convergence dilemma. In K. Crenshaw, N. Gotanda, G. Peller, & K. Thomas (Eds.), *Critical race theory: The key writings that formed the movement* (pp. 20–28). New York: New Press.

Bennett, W. (2003, April 13). Paige's values are America's values. *The Washington Post,* B07.

Bennett, W.J., Fair, W., Finn, C.E., Jr., Flake, F., Hirsch, E.D., Marshall, W., et al. (1998). *A nation still at risk.* Washington, DC: The Heritage Foundation.

Blaxall, J., & Willows, D.M. (1984). Reading ability and text difficulty as influences on second graders' oral reading errors. *Journal of Educational Psychology, 76*(2), 330–341.

Brandt, D. (2001). *Literacy in American lives.* London: Cambridge University Press.

Brown v. Board of Educ., 347 U.S. 483 (1954).

Calkins, L.M (1994). *The art of teaching writing.* Portsmouth, NH: Heinemann.

Callahan, R.E. (1962). *Education and the cult of efficiency.* Chicago: University of Chicago Press.

Cambourne, B. (2000). Observing literacy learning in elementary classrooms: Nine years of classroom anthropology. *The Reading Teacher, 53,* 512–515.

Charter School Expansion Act of 1998, Pub. L. No. 105-278, 112 Stat. 2682 (2000).

Chomsky, N. (1979). *Language and responsibility: Based on conversations with Mitson Ronat.* New York: Knopf.

Chomsky, N. (with Macedo, D., Ed.). (2000). *Chomsky on miseducation.* Boulder, CO: Rowman & Littlefield.

Civil Rights Act of 1964, 42 U.S.C. § 2000e *et seq.*

Clay, M. (1990, April). *Reading Recovery in the United States: Its successes and challenges.* Paper presented at the American Educational Research Association, Boston, MA. (ERIC Document Reproduction Service No. ED320125)

Clegg, S.R. (1989). *Frameworks of power.* London: Sage.

Clinton, W.J., & Gore, A., Jr. (1992). *Putting people first: How we can all change America.* New York: Times Books.

Coburn, C.E. (2001). Collective sensemaking about reading: How teachers mediate reading policy in their professional communities. *Educational Evaluation and Policy Analysis, 23*(2), 145–170.

Coles, G. (2003). *Reading the naked truth: Literacy, legislation, and lies.* Portsmouth, NH: Heinemann.

Compton-Lilly, C. (2003). *Reading families: The literate lives of urban children and their families.* New York: Teachers College Press.

Cook-Gumperz, J. (1986). *The social construction of literacy.* New York: Cambridge University Press.

Cope, B., & Kalantzis, M. (2000). *Multiliteracies: Literacy learning and the design of social futures.* London: Routledge.

Cunningham, J.W. (2001). Essay book review: The National Reading Panel Report. *Reading Research Quarterly, 36,* 326–335.

Dahl, R.A. (1967). *Pluralist democracy in the United States: Conflict and consent.* Chicago: Rand McNally.

Delpit, L.D. (1995). *Other people's children: Cultural conflict in the classroom.* New York: New Press.

DeMarrais, K.B., & LeCompte, M. (1990). *Ways schools work: A sociological analysis of education.* White Plains, NY: Longman.

Dewey, J. (1916). *Democracy and education.* New York: Free Press.

Dodge, K.A., Putallaz, M., & Malone, D. (2002). Coming of age: The Department of Education. *Phi Delta Kappan, 83*(9), 674–676.

Dudziak, M.L. (1995). Desegregation as Cold War imperative. In R. Delgado (Ed.), *Critical race theory: The cutting edge* (pp. 106–117). Philadelphia: Temple University Press.

Eagleton, T. (1991). *Ideology: An introduction.* London: Verso.

Edmondson, J. (2000). *America Reads: A critical policy analysis.* Newark, DE: International Reading Association.

Edmondson, J. (2002). Asking different questions: Critical analyses and reading research *Reading Research Quarterly, 37,* 113–119.

Edmondson, J. (2003). *Prairie Town: Redefining rural life in the age of globalization.* Boulder, CO: Rowman & Littlefield.

Edmondson, J., & Shannon, P. (1998). Reading poverty and education: Questioning the reading success equation. *The Peabody Journal of Education, 73,* 104–126.

Edmondson, J., & Shannon, P. (2002). The will of the people. *The Reading Teacher, 55,* 452–454.

Edmondson, J., & Shannon, P. (2003). Reading First in rural Pennsylvania schools. *Journal of Research in Rural Education, 18*(1), 31–34.

Education Consolidation Improvement Act of 1981, Pub. L. No. 97-35, 95 Stat. 357.

Educational Excellence for All Children Act of 1999, H.R.1960, 106 Cong., 1999.

Ehri, L.C. (1978). Beginning reading from a psycholinguistic perspective: Amalgamation of word identities. In F.B. Murray (Ed.), *The recognition of words* (IRA series on the development of the reading process). Newark, DE: International Reading Association.

Ehri, L.C. (1987). Learning to read and spell words. *Journal of Reading Behavior, 19*(1), 5–31.

Ehri, L.C. (1998). Grapheme-phoneme knowledge is essential for learning to read words in English. In J.L. Metsala & L.C. Ehri (Eds.), *Word recognition in beginning literacy,* (pp. 3–40). Mahwah, NJ: Erlbaum.

Ehri, L.C., Deffner, N., & Wilce, L. (1984). Pictorial mnemonics for phonics. *Journal of Educational Psychology, 76*(5), 880–893.

Elementary and Secondary Education Act of 1965, 20 U.S.C. 6301 *et seq.*

Faith in the public sphere. (2003, April 11). *The New York Times,* p. A24.

Feuer, M. (2002, February 6). *The logic and the basic principles of scientific based research.* Paper presented at The Use of Scientifically Based Research in Education: Working Group Conference, Washington, DC. Retrieved March 27, 2002, from http://www.excelgov.org/displayContent.asp?Keyword=prppcEvidence#agenda

Finders, M. (1997). *Just girls: Hidden literacies and life in junior high* (Language and Literacy series). Urbana, IL: National Council of Teachers of English.

Fletcher, J.M., Shaywitz, S.E., Shankweiler, D.P., Katz, L., Liberman, I.Y., Stuebing, K.K., et al. (1994). Cognitive profiles of reading disability: Comparisons of discrepancy and low achievement definitions. *Journal of Educational Psychology, 86,* 6–23.

Foorman, B., Francis, D., Shaywitz, S., Shaywitz, B., & Fletcher, J. (1997). The case for early reading intervention. In B. Blachman (Ed.), *Foundations of reading acquisition and dyslexia: Implications for early intervention* (pp. 243–264). Hillsdale, NJ: Erlbaum.

Foucault, M. (with Gordon, C., Ed.). (1980). *Power-knowledge: Selected interviews and other writing, 1972–1977.* New York: Pantheon.

Fountas, I.C., & Pinnell, G.S. (1996). *Guided reading: Good first teaching for all children.* Portsmouth, NH: Heinemann.

Fraatz, J.M.B. (1987). *The politics of reading.* New York: Teachers College Press.

Francis, D.J., Shaywitz, S.E., Stuebing, K.K., Shaywitz, B.H., & Fletcher, J.M. (1996). Developmental lag versus deficit models of reading disability: A longitudinal, individual grown curves analysis. *Journal of Educational Psychology, 88,* 3–17.

Fraser, N. (1996). *Justice interruptus: Critical reflections on the "postsocialist" condition.* New York: Routledge.

Freire, P. (1972). *The pedagogy of the oppressed* (D. Macedo, Trans.). New York: Penguin.

Fullerton, S., & DeFord, D. (2001). Conversations before writing during Reading Recovery lessons: Negotiation or tug of war? In J.V. Hoffman (Ed.), *50th Yearbook of the National Reading Conference* (pp. 213–227). Chicago: National Reading Conference.

Garan, E.M. (2002). *Resisting reading mandates: How to triumph with the truth.* Portsmouth, NH: Heinemann.

Gee, J., Hull, G., & Lankshear, C. (1997). *The new work order: Behind the language of the new capitalism.* Boulder, CO: Westview Press.

Gerson, M. (1996). *The neoconservative vision: From the cold war to the culture wars.* Lanham, MD: Rowman & Littlefield.

Giroux, H.A. (1988). *Schooling and the struggle for public life: Critical pedagogy in the modern age.* Minneapolis: University of Minnesota Press.

Giroux, H.A. (2001a). *Public spaces, private lives: Beyond the culture of cynicism.* Lanham, MD: Rowman & Littlefield.

Giroux, H.A. (2001b). *Theory and resistance in education: Toward a pedagogy for the opposition* (Rev. ed.). Westport, CT: Greenwood.

Giroux, H.A. (2002). Educated hope in an age of privatized visions. *Cultural Studies Critical Methodologies, 2*(1), 93–112.

Giroux, H.A. (2003). *The abandoned generation: Democracy beyond the culture of fear.* New York: Palgrave MacMillan.

Goals 2000: Educate America Act of 1994, Pub. L. No. 103-227, 108 Stat. 125 (1996).

Gold, D.L. (1987, November 25). $2.5-billion child-care proposal unveiled. *Education Week.* Retrieved May 26, 2003, from http://www.edweek.org

Gonzalez, R.D., & Melis, I. (2000). *Language ideologies: Critical perspectives on the official English movement: Education and the social implications of official language.* Mahwah, NJ: Erlbaum.

Goodman, W. (2001). *Living and teaching in an unjust world: New perspectives on multicultural education.* Portsmouth, NH: Heinemann.

Goodnough, A. (2003a, January 24). Bush adviser casts doubt on the benefits of phonics program. *The New York Times,* p. B1.

Goodnough, A. (2003b, April 5). More intensive reading program is added for struggling pupils. *The New York Times,* p. D1.

Gordon, D.M. (1996). *Fat and mean: The corporate squeeze of working America and the myth of managerial "downsizing."* New York: Free Press.

Harding, V., Kelley, R.D.G., & Lewis, E. (2000). We changed the world. In R.D.G. Kelley & E. Lewis (Eds.), *To make our world anew: A history of African Americans* (pp. 445–542). New York: Oxford University Press.

Harvey, D. (2000). *Spaces of hope.* Berkeley: University of California Press.

Heath, S.B. (1983). *Ways with words: Language, life, and work in communities and classrooms.* Cambridge, UK: Cambridge University Press.

Heclo, H. (1978). Issue networks and executive establishment. In A. King (Ed.), *The new American political system* (pp. 87–124). Washington, DC: American Enterprise Institute for Public Policy Research.

Henwood, G.F. (1999/2000). A new role for the reading specialist: Contributing toward a high school's collaborative educational culture. *Journal of Adolescent & Adult Literacy, 43,* 316–325.

Hochschild, J. (2001, Fall). Public schools and the American Dream. *Dissent,* 35–42.

Horkheimer, M. (1974). *Critique of instrumental reason: Lectures and essays since the end of World War II.* New York: The Seabury Press.

Improving America's Schools Act of 1994, Pub. L. No. 103-382, 108 Stat. 3632 (1996).

Jaegar, E.L. (1996). The reading specialist as collaborative consultant. *The Reading Teacher, 49,* 622–629.

Jennings, J.F. (1995, January 11). What to expect from a new year and a new Congress. *Education Week.* Retrieved April 30, 2003, from http://www.edweek.org

Jennings, J.F. (2000). Title I: Its legislative history and its promise. *Phi Delta Kappan, 81*(7), 516–522.

Johnson, L.B. (1964, May 22). *The Great Society.* Retrieved October 21, 2002, from http://www.tamu.edu/comm/prcs/speeches/lbjgreat.html

Kaestle, C.F., & Smith, M.S. (1982). The federal role in elementary and secondary education, 1940–1980. *Harvard Educational Review, 52*(4), 384–408.

Kamil, M.L., & Intrator, S. (1998). Quantitative trends in publication of research on technology and reading, writing, and literacy. In T. Shanahan, F.V. Rodriguez-Brown, C. Wortham, J.C. Burnison, & A. Cheung (Eds.), *47th Yearbook of the National Reading Conference* (pp. 385–396). Chicago: National Reading Conference.

Kamil, M.L., Intrator, S., & Kim, H.S. (2000). Effects of other technologies on literacy and literacy learning. In M.L. Kamil, P.B. Mosenthal, P.D. Pearson, & R. Barr (Eds.), *Handbook of reading research* (Vol. 3, pp. 773–788). Mahwah, NJ: Erlbaum.

Kamil, M.L., & Lane, D. (1998). Researching the relation between technology and literacy: An agenda for the 21st century. In D. Reinking, M.C. McKenna, L.D. Labbo, & R.D. Kieffer (Eds.), *Handbook of literacy and technology: Transformations in a post-typographic world* (pp. 323–341). Mahwah, NJ: Erlbaum.

Kant, I. (1960). *Education.* Ann Arbor: University of Michigan Press.

Kantor, H. (1991). Education, social reform, and the state: ESEA and federal education policy in the 1960s. *American Journal of Education, 100*(1), 47–83.

Kantor, H., & Lowe, R. (1995). Class, race, and the emergence of federal education policy: From the New Deal to the Great Society. *Educational Researcher, 24*(3), 4–11, 21.

Kohn, A. (2002). Students don't "work"—they learn. In A. Kohn & P. Shannon (Eds.), *Education, Inc.: Turning learning into a business* (Rev. ed., pp. 63–66). Portsmouth, NH: Heinemann.

Kohn, A., & Shannon, P. (2002). *Education, Inc.: Turning learning into a business* (Rev. ed.). Portsmouth, NH: Heinemann.

Kozol, J. (1991). *Savage inequalities: Children in America's schools.* New York: Crown.

Krashen, S. (2000, May 10). Reading report: One researcher's "errors and omissions" [Electronic version]. *Education Week, 19*(35), 48–50.

Kristol, I. (1995). *Neoconservativism: Selected essays 1949–1995.* New York: Free Press.

Ladson-Billings, G., & Tate, W. (1995). Toward a critical race theory of education. *Teachers College Record, 97*(1), 47–68.

Lagemann, E.C. (2000). *An elusive science: The troubling history of education research.* Chicago: University of Chicago Press.

Lehmbruch, G. & Schmitter, P. (Eds). (1980). *Patterns of corporatist policy-making.* London: Sage.

Lowi, T.J. (1964). American business, public policy, case studies, and political theory. *World Politics, 16,* 677–715.

Lowi, T.J. (1979). *The end of liberalism: The second republic of the United States* (2nd ed.). New York: W.W. Norton.

Magliano, J.P., Trabasso, T., & Graesser, A.C. (1999). Strategic processing during comprehension. *Journal of Educational Psychology, 91*(4), 615–629.

Marcuse, H. (2001). The individual in the Great Society. In D. Kellner (Ed.), *Towards a critical theory of society: Herbert Marcuse* (pp. 59–80). New York: Routledge.

Marshall, C. (1997). *Feminist critical policy analysis I: A perspective from primary and secondary schooling.* London: Falmer.

Marx, K. (1963). *The 18th Brumiere of Louis Bonaparte.* New York: International. (Original work published 1852)

Marx, K. (with Engels, F.). (1998). *The German ideology: Including thesis on Feuerbach and introduction to the critique of political economy.* New York: Prometheus. (Original work published 1932)

McClellan, D. (Ed.). (2000). *Karl Marx: Selected writings.* New York: Oxford University Press.

McGill-Franzen, A. (2000). Policy and instruction: What is the relationship? In M.L. Kamil, P.B. Mosenthal, P.D. Pearson, & R. Barr (Eds.), *Handbook of reading research* (Vol. 3, pp. 889–908). Mahwah, NJ: Erlbaum.

Mendez, G. (2001). Identity and difference in textbooks and life. In P. Shannon (Ed.), *Becoming political, too: New readings and writings on the politics of literacy education* (pp. 237–245). Portsmouth, NH: Heinemann.

Metcalf, S. (2002, January 28). Reading between the lines. *The Nation,* pp. 18–22.

Miliband, R. (1969). *State in capitalist society: An analysis of the Western system of power.* New York: Basic Books.

Mills, C.W. (1956). *The power elite.* London: Oxford University Press.

Mills, C.W. (1959). *The sociological imagination.* London: Oxford University Press.

Monaghan, E.J., & Saul, E.W. (1987). The reader, the scribe, the thinker: A critical look at the history of American reading and writing instruction. In T.S. Popkewitz (Ed.), *The formation of school subjects: The struggle for creating an American institution* (pp. 85–122). London: Taylor & Francis.

Mouffe, C. (1995). Politics, democratic action, and solidarity. *Inquiry, 38,* 99–108.

National Commission on Excellence in Education. (1983). *A nation at risk: The imperative for educational reform.* Washington, DC: U.S. Department of Education.

National Institute of Child Health and Human Development (NICHD). (2000). *Report of the National Reading Panel. Teaching children to read: An evidence-based assessment of the scientific research literature on reading and its implications for reading instruction* (NIH Publication No. 00-4769). Washington, DC: U.S. Government Printing Office.

National Reading Panel. (1998a, April 24). [National Reading Panel Meeting]. Unpublished transcript.

National Reading Panel. (1998b, July 24). [National Reading Panel Meeting]. Unpublished transcript.

National Reading Panel. (1999a, October 13). [National Reading Panel Meeting]. Unpublished transcript.

National Reading Panel. (1999b, October 14). [National Reading Panel Meeting]. Unpublished transcript.

Nealon, J.T., & Giroux, S.S. (2003). *The theory toolbox: Critical concepts for the humanities, arts, and social sciences.* Lanham, MD: Rowman & Littlefield.

Newton, K. (1969). A critique of the pluralist model. *Acta Sociologica, 12,* 209–243.

No Child Left Behind Act of 2001, Pub. L. No. 107-110, 115 Stat. 1425 (2003).

Noble, D. (1994). Let them eat skills. *The Review of Education/Pedagogy/Cultural Studies, 16*(1), 15–29.

Orfield, G., & Wald, J. (2000, June 5). Testing, testing. *The Nation,* pp. 38–40.

Powell, R.L. (1999). *Literacy as a moral imperative: Facing the challenges of a pluralistic society.* Lanham, MD: Rowman & Littlefield.

Prendergast, C.C. (2002). The economy of literacy: How the Supreme Court stalled the Civil Rights movement. *Harvard Educational Review, 72*(2), 206–229.

Prendergast, C.C. (2003). *Literacy and racial justice: The politics of learning after* Brown v. Board of Education. Carbondale: Southern Illinois University Press.

Prunty, J.J. (1985). Signposts for a critical educational policy analysis. *Australian Journal of Education, 29*(2), 133–140.

Public Agenda. (2003). *Where we are now: 12 things you need to know about public opinion and public schools.* Retrieved January 11, 2003, from http://www.publicagenda.org/specials/wherewearenow/wherewearenow.htm

Quatroche, D.J., Bean, R.M., & Hamilton, R.L. (2001). The role of the reading specialist: A review of research. *The Reading Teacher, 55,* 282–294.

Reading Excellence Act of 1998, 20 U.S.C. § 6661 *et seq.*

Reading Recovery Council of North America (2003). [Homepage]. Retrieved April 4, 2003, from http://www.readingrecovery.org

Reich, R.B. (2001). *The future of success.* New York: Knopf.

Reyna, V. (2002, February 6). *What is scientifically based evidence? What is its logic?* Paper presented at The Use of Scientifically Based Research in Education: Working Group Conference, Washington, DC. Retrieved March 27, 2003, from http://www.excel gov.org/displayContent.asp?Keyword=prppcEvidence#agenda

Robelon, E. (2002, January 9). An ESEA primer [Electronic version]. *Education Week, 21*(6), 28–29.

Roller, C.M., & Long, R.M. (2001). Critical issues: Sounding like more than background noise to policy makers: Qualitative researchers in the policy arena. *Journal of Literacy Research, 33*(4), 707–725.

Ross, E.W., & Mathison, S. (2002, March). No child left untested? *Z Magazine, 15*(3), 14–15.

Routman, R. (1988). *Transitions: From literature to literacy.* Portsmouth, NH: Heinemann.

Salkind, N.J. (2000). *Exploring research* (4th ed.). Upper Saddle River, NJ: Prentice Hall.

Saltman, K. (2003). *Education, Inc.* [Book review]. Retrieved May 6, 2003, from http://www.tcrecord.org

Samuels, S.J. (1979). The method of repeated readings. *The Reading Teacher, 32,* 403–408.

Samuels, S.J., & Kamil, M.L. (1984). Models of the reading process. In P.D. Pearson, R. Barr, M.L. Kamil, & P. Mosenthal (Eds.), *Handbook of reading research* (pp. 185–221). New York: Longman.

Samuels, S.J., LaBerge, D., & Bremer, C. (1978). Units of word recognition: Evidence for developmental changes. *Journal of Verbal Learning and Verbal Behavior, 17*(6), 715–720.

Samuels, S.J., Miller, N., & Eisenberg, P. (1979). Practice effects on the unit of word recognition. *Journal of Educational Psychology, 71*(4), 514–520.

Schneider, A.L., & Ingram, H. (1997). *Policy design for democracy.* Lawrence: University of Kansas Press.

Shanahan, T. (1994). Assumptions underlying educational intervention research: A commentary on Harris and Pressley. *Educational Psychology Review, 6,* 255–262.

Shanahan, T. (1997). Reading-writing relationships, thematic units, inquiry learning…In pursuit of effective integrated literacy instruction. *The Reading Teacher, 51,* 12–19.

Shanahan, T., & Neuman, S.B. (1997). Literacy research that makes a difference. *Reading Research Quarterly, 32,* 202–210.

Shannon, P. (1989). *Broken promises: Reading instruction in twentieth-century America.* Westport, CT: Greenwood.

Shannon, P. (1990). *The struggle to continue: Progressive reading instruction in the United States.* Portsmouth, NH: Heinemann.

Shannon, P. (1991). Politics, policy, and reading research. In R. Barr, M.L. Kamil, P.B. Mosenthal, & P.D. Pearson (Eds.), *Handbook of reading research* (Vol. 2, pp. 147–167). New York: Longman.

Shannon, P. (1998). *Reading poverty.* Portsmouth, NH: Heinemann.

Shannon, P. (2000). "What's my name?": A politics of literacy in the latter half of the 20th century in America. *Reading Research Quarterly, 35,* 90–107.

Shannon, P. (2002a). Hog farms in Pennsylvania. *The Reading Teacher, 56,* 688–690.

Shannon, P. (2002b). Philadelphia freedom. *The Reading Teacher, 56,* 48–50.

Shannon, P., Edmondson, J., & O'Brien, S. (2002). Expressions of power and ideology in the National Reading Panel: A study in consensus building. In T. Shanahan (Ed.), *51st Yearbook of the National Reading Conference* (pp. 383–395). Chicago: National Reading Conference.

Shavelson, R.J., & Towne, L. (Eds.). (2002). *Scientific research in education.* Washington, DC: National Academy Press.

Siegel, M., & Fernandez, S. (2000). Critical approaches. In M.L. Kamil, P.B. Mosenthal, P.D. Pearson, & R. Barr (Eds.), *Handbook of reading research* (Vol. 3, pp. 141–152). Mahwah, NJ: Erlbaum.

Smith, F. (2003). *Unspeakable acts, unnatural practices: Flaws and fallacies in "scientific" reading instruction.* Portsmouth, NH: Heinemann.

Smith, M.S., & Scoll, B.W. (1995). The Clinton human capital agenda. *Teachers College Record, 96*(3), 389–404.

Snow, C., Burns, S., & Griffin, P. (1998). *Preventing reading difficulties in young children.* Washington, DC: National Academy Press.

Sorel, E., & Lingeman, R. (2003, June 30). Religion in the news. *The Nation,* p. 7.

Street, B.V. (1995). *Social literacies: Critical approaches to literacy in development, ethnography, and education.* New York: Longman.

Taylor, D. (1998). *Beginning to read and the spin doctors of science: The political campaign to change America's mind about how children learn to read.* Urbana, IL: National Council of Teachers of English.

Theodoulou, S., & Cahn, M. (1995). *Public policy: The essential readings.* Englewood Cliffs, NJ: Prentice Hall.

Truman, D.B. (1971). *The governmental process: Political interests and public opinions* (2nd ed.). New York: Knopf.

Tyack, D. (1991). Public school reform: Policy talk and institutional practice. *American Journal of Education, 100*(1), 1–19.

Tyack, D.B., & Cuban, L. (1995). *Tinkering toward utopia: A century of public school reform.* Cambridge, MA: Harvard University Press.

US Charter Schools. (2003, November 19). *Overview.* Retrieved from http://www.uscharter schools.org/pub/uscs_docs/o/index.htm

U.S. Department of Education. (2001, December 4). *Secretary Paige applauds recipients of prestigious 2001 Malcom Baldrige National Quality Award: Three education organizations are the first-ever winners in the education category* [Press release]. Retrieved April 17, 2003, from http://www.ed.gov/PressReleases/12-2001/12042001b.html

Vacca, J.L., & Padak, N.D. (1990). Reading consultants as classroom collaborators: An emerging role. *Journal of Educational and Psychological Consultations, 1*(1), 99–107.

Vogt, M., & Shearer, B.A. (2003). *Reading specialists in the real world: A sociocultural view.* Boston: Allyn & Bacon.

Watson, C., & Willows, D.M. (1995). Information-processing patterns in specific reading disability. *Journal of Learning Disabilities, 28*(4), 216–231.

Williams, J.P. (1993). Comprehension of students with and without learning disabilities: Identification of narrative themes and idiosyncratic text representations. *Journal of Educational Psychology, 85*(4), 631–641.

Williams, J.P. (1998). Improving the comprehension of disabled readers. *Annals of Dyslexia, 68*, 213–238.

Williams, J.P., Brown, L.G., & Silverstein, A. (1994). An instructional program in comprehension of narrative themes for adolescents with learning disabilities. *Learning Disability Quarterly, 17*(3), 205–221.

Willows, D.M., & Ryan, E.B. (1986). The development of grammatical sensitivity and its relationship to early reading achievement. *Reading Research Quarterly, 21*, 253–266.

INDEX

Page references followed by *f* or *t* indicate figures or tables, respectively.

F

G

H